Sustainable Health Insurance Model:

Policy Options for Low and Middle-Income Countries, Evidence from Ghana

Sustainable Health Insurance Model:

Policy Options for Low and Middle-Income Countries, Evidence from Ghana

Abass Suleymana

ISBN: 978-81-19524-13-6

First published in India in 2024 by Exceller Books,
An imprint of GE Group

Address: G1, Dream Apartment, Degree College Road, Belgharia,
Kolkata, 700056, India

www.excellerbooks.com

Acknowledgement

I deeply thank Rahilu Haruna, my beautiful wife, for reviewing the manuscript and providing constructive criticism.

I would also like to express my genuine appreciation to the Executive Management of the NHIA, the Staff of the Upper West Region of the Authority, and the Staff of the Research, Policy, Monitoring and Evaluation Directorate of the NHIA for their invaluable advice and encouragement.

Furthermore, I am grateful to Exceller Books global publishing house for their excellent professionalism.

Last but not least, I thank my dear wife, Rahilu, and my children, Nina and Ayan, for their kind support and cooperation throughout the duration of this project. I say a big thank you to them.

Acronyms

CHE	Current Health Expenditure
CHPS	Community-Based Health Planning Services
CSO	Civil Society Organization
DMHIS	District-Wide Mutual Health Insurance Scheme
DRG	Diagnostics Related Grouping
FFS	Fee For Service
GDP	Gross Domestic Products
G-DRG	Ghana Diagnostics Related Grouping
GGE	General Government Expenditure
GGHE-D	General Domestic Government Expenditure
HIPC	Highly Indebted Poor Country
HRH	Human Resource For Health
LI	Legislative Instrument
MOH	Ministry Of Health
NHIA	National Health Insurance Authority
NHIL	National Health Insurance Levy
NHIS	National Health Insurance Scheme
OPD	Outpatient Department
OPP	Out Of Pocket Payment
PHC	Primary Health Care
PHIS	Private Health Insurance Scheme
SSNIT	Social Security And National Insurance Trust
UHC	Universal Health Coverage
WHO	World Health Organisation

Executive Summary

Ghana has an integrated health system, with all the building blocks interacting with one another, contributing significantly to improving access to health care, ensuring financial risk protection, and improving quality of care. Over the years, Ghana has made significant progress in the health sector through interventions designed to achieve health-related Sustainable Development Goals (SDGs), among other things.

One of the remarkable achievements of the health sector is the establishment of the National Health Insurance Scheme (NHIS) in 2003; which seeks to provide financial risks protection to persons living in Ghana; particularly to the poor and the disadvantaged in society. Until the establishment of the NHIS, the provision of health care in Ghana was based on user charges popularly known as "cash and carry". The NHIS's primary objective is to provide financial risk protection against the costs of healthcare expenditure for all residents in Ghana. This is anchored on the principles of equity, solidarity, risk-sharing, cross-subsidization, and community ownership (MOH, 2004). About 20 years since its introduction, the NHIS has grown from strength to strength. It has become a model of healthcare financing in Africa and for many low-and-middle-income countries around the globe. This book, therefore, seeks to present the anatomy of the National Health Insurance Scheme in Ghana.

The work relied on secondary information from various sources, such as published books and articles, review papers, newspaper articles, existing studies, and ongoing discussions on the processes, lessons, achievements, challenges, and direction of reforms of Ghana's National Health Insurance Scheme.

In line with the health financing functions of revenue collection, risk pooling and purchasing, the book highlights the sources of funds to the NHIS, how the fund is pooled to ensure equity in healthcare financing and how healthcare services are purchased using the pooled funds. Finally, the book aims to proffer recommendations for low- and middle-income countries regarding policy options for a sustainable health insurance model, using evidence from Ghana's NHIS.

Table of Contents

List of Figures

List of Tables

Chapter 1
Introduction

This chapter outlines the background of Ghana and the rationale for this book, the methodology used, the limitations of the work, the conceptual framework, and the book's structure.

1.1. Background and Rationale

The Republic of Ghana is located on the West African Coast. It is bordered by Togo on the east, Burkina Faso on the north, and Côte d'Ivoire on the west. The Gulf of Guinea lies to the south. Ghana has sixteen administrative regions (figure 1).

Figure 1: Administrative Map of Ghana

These are Ashanti, Bono, Bono East, Ahafo, Central, Eastern, Greater Accra, Northern, Savanna, North East, Upper East, Upper West, Volta, Oti, Western and Western North. The country has a total land area of 238,537 square kilometres. Ghana has a tropical climate, characterised most of the year by moderate temperatures of 21-32°C, constant breezes and sunshine. It has a wet and dry season, but it is mainly warm and dry in the southeast, hot and humid in the southwest and hot and dry in the north. Annual rainfall ranges from about 1,015 millimetres in the North to about 2,030 millimetres in the south.

Ghana was called the Gold Coast. The name Gold Coast came from the early Europeans due to the abundant gold traded on the country's coast. After independence, the name 'Gold Coast' was legally changed to Ghana. Osagyefo Dr Kwame Nkrumah became the first President of Ghana after independence on 6th March 1957. The country became a republic in the British Commonwealth of Nations on 1st July 1960. Ghana practices a multi-party democratic presidential system of government with an Executive Presidency elected for four years with a maximum of two terms. Parliament and the Judiciary constitute the other two arms of government. Parliamentarians are elected every four years. Ghana has vibrant media and civil society organisations independent of the three arms of government.

According to the 2021 Population and Housing Census (PHC) report, Ghana's population stood at 30,832,019 (GSS, 2021). This is made up of 15,200,440 males (49.3%) and 15,631,579 females (50.7%). Ghana has one of the highest GDPs per capita in West Africa and is ranked as a lower-middle economy by the World Bank. The country has a diverse and rich resource base, with gold, cocoa, timber, diamond, bauxite, and manganese being the most important sources of foreign trade. In 2007, Ghana discovered an oilfield. By 2010, the country had commenced the production of oil in commercial quantities, qualifying her to be counted among the league of oil-producing countries. Until 2006, Ghana's economy was dominated by agriculture, but it's now led by the service sector, accounting for about 47.2% of national output in 2019. Agriculture accounted for about 18.5 per cent in 2019, while industry accounted for about 34.2% of total national output. Provisional GDP estimates for 2019 showed a growth rate of 6.5 per cent compared to 6.3 per cent in 2018. The Services sector recorded the highest growth rate of 7.6 per cent, followed by Industry (6.4%) and Agriculture (4.6%) sectors (GSS, 2020).

Ghana has an integrated health system with all the building blocks of the health system interacting with one another, contributing significantly to improving access to health care, ensuring financial risk protection, and improving quality of care. Over the years, significant progress has been made in the health sector through interventions that are designed to achieve health-related Sustainable Development Goals (SDGs). Various health-related measures like improving health infrastructure, offering financial risk protection, and boosting the healthcare workforce have led to positive changes in health outcomes. For instance, maternal mortality dropped from 634 per 100,000 live births in 1990 to 119 per 100,000 live births in 2021. Similarly, the infant mortality rate decreased from 77 per 1,000 live births in 1988 to about 8 per 1,000 live births in 2021, and the under-5 mortality rate went down from 155 per 1,000 live births in 1988 to about 11 per 1,000 live births in 2021.

The number of women dying due to complications from pregnancy or childbirth has improved over the last five years. According to the 2021 holistic assessment report of the Ministry of Health Ghana, the institutional maternal mortality ratio declined from 147 to 119.5 per 100,000 live births between 2017 and 2021. Stillbirth, neonatal mortality, infant mortality, and under-5 mortality have all assumed upward trends but remained relatively low (MOH, 2022).

One of the remarkable achievements of the health sector was the establishment of the National Health Insurance Scheme (NHIS) in 2003, which sought to provide financial risk protection to persons living in Ghana, particularly to the poor and the disadvantaged in society. Until the establishment of the NHIS, the provision of health care in Ghana was based on user charges popularly known as "cash and carry". Under the cash and carry system, patients were made to pay for their healthcare needs at the point of service use. Since then, successive governments have recognized the need to undo the 'cash and carry' system because it provides a disincentive to the utilization of health care, especially among the poor and vulnerable in society. The NHIS was therefore established as a social protection initiative to remedy the menace of the 'cash and carry' system. The NHIS's primary objective is to provide financial risk protection against the costs of healthcare expenditure for all residents in Ghana. This is anchored on the principles of equity, solidarity, risk-sharing, cross-subsidization, and community ownership (MOH, 2004). Over the years, the NHIS has grown from strength to strength. It has become a model of healthcare financing in Africa and for many low-and-middle-income countries around the globe.

This book, therefore, seeks to present the anatomy of the National Health Insurance Scheme in Ghana. In line with the health financing functions of revenue collection, risk pooling and purchasing, the book seeks to highlight the sources of funds to the NHIS, how the fund is pooled to ensure equity in health financing and how healthcare services are purchased using the pooled funds. Finally, the book aims to proffer recommendations for low-and middle-income countries regarding policy options for a sustainable health insurance model using evidence from Ghana's NHIS.

1.2. Methodology

The work relied on secondary information from various sources i.e. published books and articles, review papers, newspaper articles, existing studies and ongoing discussions on the processes, lessons, achievements, challenges and direction of reforms of Ghana's National Health Insurance Scheme.

Existing literature on legislations and regulations regarding the establishment, implementation and operations of the National Health Insurance Scheme were accessed and analysed. Quantitative data from several sources was accessed and analysed. These sources included published reports from the National Health Insurance Authority, the Ghana Statistical Service, Ghana's Ministry of Health, Ghana Health Service, and the School of Public Health of the University of Ghana, the National Development Planning Commission of Ghana, International Labour Organisation, and the World Health Organization.

1.3. Limitations

This work primarily used secondary information. Ghana's Health Insurance Scheme is relatively young, about two decades old, which made it a little difficult to draw ample literature on the subject matter. However, grey literature was reviewed to complement the inadequacy therein. Quality checks were done through credible websites to mitigate this effect.

1.4. Conceptual Framework

The conceptual framework (figure 2) that underpins this work is adapted from the work of Carrin G and James C (2005). The work mirrors the three main functions of health financing: (1) revenue collection, (2) risk pooling, and (3) purchasing. It asks the far-reaching questions of how revenue should be collected from different sources to finance the healthcare of the people (revenue collection); how should the collected funds be put together in a pool so that the risk of having to pay for health care is not borne individually (risk pooling); and how should the pooled funds be used to pay providers for delivering a defined package of health services and products (purchasing).

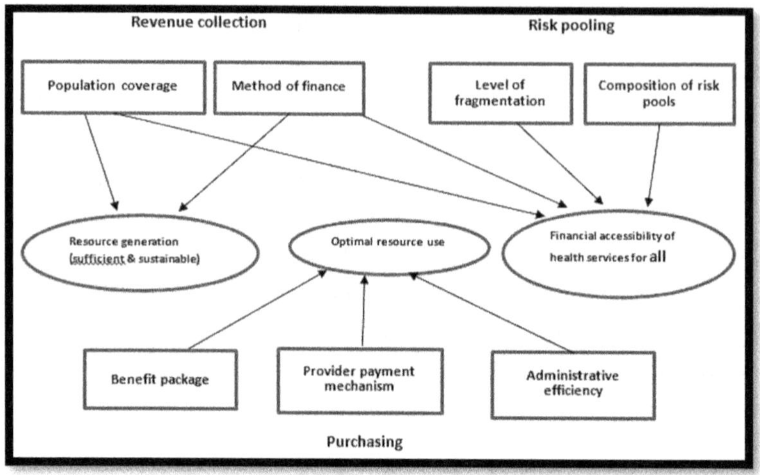

Figure 2: Key Design Issues in Health Financing
Source: Carrin G and James C, 2005

Figure 3 illustrates the key design framework, showing the three (3) main health financing functions, the key design components and questions that underpin Ghana's efforts in establishing, implementing and operationalizing the NHIS. This is centred around several design choices that need to be considered to achieve the health financing targets of providing sufficient and sustainable resources, accessibility of health services for all and optimal use of resources.

1.5. Structure of the Book

This book is structured in five chapters. Chapter 1 provides background information on Ghana, the rationale for this study, the methodology used, the limitations of the study, the conceptual framework and the structure of the book. Chapter 2 provides the evolution of healthcare financing in Ghana and an overview of Ghana's National Health Insurance Scheme. Chapter 3 presents the policy design components and questions underpinning the establishment, implementation and operations of Ghana's National Health Insurance Scheme. Chapter 4 analyses the performance of Ghana's National Health Insurance. Chapter 5 discusses critical policy design decisions needed for a sustainable, equitable and progressive health insurance model for low- and middle-income countries.

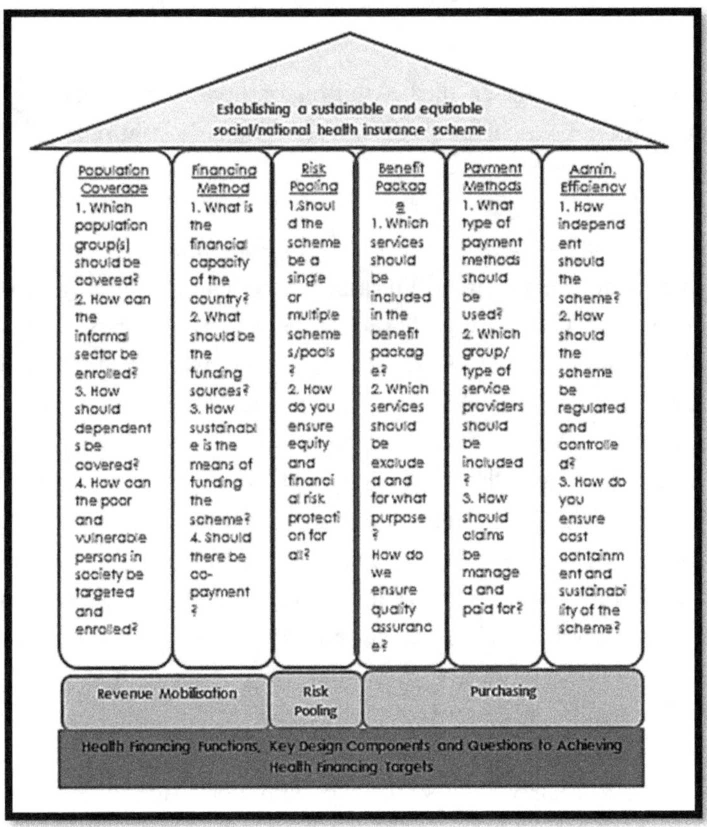

Figure 3: Key Design Components and Questions That Underpinned the Establishment, Implementation, and Operations of Ghana's NHIS
Source: Author's Own Creation

23

Chapter 2
Health Financing Arrangements in Ghana

This chapter discusses the evolution of healthcare financing in Ghana and provides an overview of Ghana's National Health Insurance Scheme.

2.1. Evolution of Health Care Financing in Ghana

According to the available literature, healthcare financing in pre-independence Ghana was based on out-of-pocket payment and public financing for expatriate civil servants (NDPC, 2009; Durairaj et al., 2010; Hendriks, 2010; Mensah et al., 2010). The literature suggests that at independence in 1957, Osagyefo Dr. Kwame Nkrumah, the first President of Ghana, introduced a policy of free education and health. Until the late 1960s, healthcare financing was free and was financed through general tax and donor support. Under this financing mechanism, Ghanaians could seek medical attention in any public health facility without having to pay out of pocket at the point of receiving health care services (NDPC 2009; Durairaj et al., 2010; Hendriks, 2010).

In the early 1970s, the Hospital Fees Act of 1971 (Act 387) was passed to provide the legal framework to introduce the fee-paying system in all public health facilities aimed at recovering costs. The fees charged were so meagre that the cost recovered was insignificant as compared to the actual cost of delivering health care services (MOH, 1971). In the mid-1970s, Ghana was faced with a general economic downturn, generally attributable to high inflation, high unemployment rates, and a huge budget deficit. By the early 1980s, the economic slowdown had worsened, which led to shortfalls in government revenue, among other adverse effects. In response to this economic downturn, an Economic Recovery Programme (ERP) was initiated in 1983 with the support of the World Bank and the International Monetary Fund (IMF). In 1983, the Government introduced the Hospital Fees Regulation (L.I. 1277) of 1983, which sought to provide policy framework and guidelines to improve upon fee collection in all public health facilities, as mandated by Act 387.

Consequent to the Bamako Initiative in 1985, a Legislative Instrument (LI) 1313 (the Hospital Fees Regulation) was introduced as a cost recovery policy that was aimed at generating at least fifteen per cent of the Ministry of Health's total recurrent expenditure in 1986, 1987 and 1989. The 1985 policy framework stipulated that:

- Patients pay fully for drugs, except in the use of specified communicable diseases such as tuberculosis, leprosy, meningitis, chicken pox, cholera, measles etc.
- Charges vary according to the level of health facilities used.
- There should be differential charges for adults and children, Ghanaian and non-Ghanaian.

L.I. 1313 was operationalized in 1986, which indicated revenue retention for part of fees collected based on the level of health care facility. Health Centers and Clinics were to retain 25 per cent of fees collected: District Hospital 50 per cent, Regional Hospital 50 per cent and Psychiatric Hospital and Leprosaria 100 per cent. However, since the beginning of 1990, all institution retained their full revenue (Waddington & Enyimayew, 1989). Under the hospital fee payment system, access and utilisation studies showed a significant reduction in the use of health services, especially in rural areas (Asenso-Okyere, 1998; Atim, 1998).

From the late 1980s through to the 1990s, the Government introduced user fees, commonly called the 'cash and carry' system, to finance healthcare in Ghana. Under this arrangement, payment was made before health care services were rendered in all public facilities. The 'cash and carry' system in Ghana undoubtedly contributed to inequitable health service access and utilisation between different socio-economic groups and between poor rural and richer urban dwellers (Waddington & Enyimayew, 1989; Nyonator & Kutzin, 1999). In response to this challenge, the Government introduced an exemption policy. The policy exempted children under the age of 5, prenatal care for pregnant women, health care services for the indigent, the elderly (those above 70 years), and disease-specific services. However, implementation was less successful, largely due to human attitudes, among others.

These problems prompted the emergence of some Mutual Health Organisations (MHO), mainly mission hospitals, as a strategy to avoid the problems associated with paying for services at the point of care (Sulzbach et al., December 2005). Nkoranza, in the Bono East region, became the soil in which the seed of MHO took root in Ghana in 1992. According to Atim (2000), the idea of starting a health insurance scheme in Nkoranza was raised at a meeting of Catholic Church hospital administrators in Sunyani in 1989. To emulate the Nkoranza model, a number of voluntary Mutual Health Organizations (MHOs) were established with the help of donor funding (ILO, 2005). By 2002, about 159 MHOs in Ghana, in 67 districts, were established (Atim et al., 2001).

According to an ILO report (2005), in 1995, a number of proposals were made in a report called 'A Feasibility Study for the Establishment of a National Health Insurance Scheme in Ghana'; however, an attempt to pilot the scheme in 1997 stalled for a variety of reasons (Atim et al., 2001). In order to realise the growth of MHOs, the Ministry of Health helped to establish a few

MHOs across the country to become models for other communities to replicate. A notable example was the establishment of an MHO in the Dangme West District in the Greater Accra Region in 1998 to test the feasibility of such schemes with the aim of nationalizing the MHOs into a health insurance scheme. The introduction of the pilot schemes saw some increases in utilization and access, promoting equity and efficiency in the areas in which these schemes existed. However, the combined total coverage they extended to the population was just one per cent (Atim, Grey, & Apoya, 2001).

To deal with the user fee challenges, low population coverage by MHOs and inequities in access to healthcare, among others, a number of political parties in Ghana captured in their manifestoes in the 2000 general elections that they would introduce health insurance schemes when voted into power. In pursuant to the above, in 2003, the Government of the New Patriotic Party (NPP) established the National Health Insurance Scheme (NHIS) through the passage of the National Health Insurance Act, 2003 (Act 650).

2.2. Ghana's NHIS in Brief

2.2.1. Background

The lack of financial protection for the citizenry (especially the poor and vulnerable in society) due to the cash and carry system triggered demand by various stakeholders, including political parties and academia, to explore alternative means of financing healthcare in the country.

During the 2000 electioneering period, a number of political parties promised that they were going to abolish the user fee system and introduce a health insurance scheme for all Ghanaians. The New Patriotic Party (NPP) led by its Presidential Candidate, Mr. John Agyekum Kufuor, won the 2000 Presidential

Elections. Mr. Kufuor was sworn into office as the 2nd President of the 4th Republic of Ghana on 7th January 2001.

In fulfilment of his campaign promise on health care financing in Ghana, Mr. Kufuor established a national health insurance team in 2001 to draft a policy framework for the introduction of a health insurance scheme, and by 2002, the first draft policy framework was developed. This policy framework metamorphosed into the National Health Insurance Bill (NHIB), which was passed into law in 2003 through an Act of Parliament (Act 650). Box 1 provides the vision and the policy objective of the government that supported the establishment of Ghana's NHIS.

> "Ultimately, the vision of government in instituting a health insurance scheme in the country is to assure equitable and universal access for all residents of Ghana to an acceptable quality package of essential healthcare, that every resident of Ghana shall belong to a health insurance scheme that adequately covers him or her against the need to pay out of pocket at the point of service use in order to obtain access to a defined package of acceptable quality of health service"

Box 1: Policy Objective of Ghana's NHIS
Source: Ministry of Health (MOH), August 2004: national health insurance policy framework for Ghana; revised edition

Act 650 (2003), as reviewed under Act 852 (2012), established an independent regulatory body called the National Health Insurance Council (NHIC), now known as the National Health Insurance Authority (NHIA). Also, the Act established the National Health Insurance Fund (NHIF) through the imposition of the National Health Insurance Levy (NHIL). The objective of the NHIA was to secure the implementation of a national health insurance policy that ensures access to basic healthcare services for all residents. As part of its functions, the Authority shall register, license and regulate health insurance schemes; supervise the operations of health insurance schemes; grant accreditation to healthcare providers; and monitor their performance (box 2).

To achieve the object of the Authority, the Authority shall

(a) implement, operate and manage the National Health Insurance Scheme;

(b) determine in consultation with the Minister contributions that should be made by members of the National Health Insurance Scheme;

(c) register members of the National Health Insurance Scheme;

(d) register and supervise private health insurance schemes;

(e) issue identity cards to members of the National Health Insurance Scheme;

(f) ensure:

    (i) equity in health care coverage

    (ii) access by the poor to healthcare services

    (iii) protection of the' poor ,and vulnerable against financial risk;

(g) grant credentials to healthcare providers and facilities that provide healthcare services to members of the National Health Insurance Scheme;

(h) manage the National Health Insurance Fund;

(i) provide a decentralised system to receive and resolve complaints by members of the National Health Insurance Scheme and healthcare providers;

(j) receive, process and pay claims for services rendered by healthcare providers;

(k) undertake public education on health insurance on its own or in collaboration with other bodies;

(l) make proposals to the Minister for the formulation of policies on health insurance;

(m) undertake programmes that further the sustainability of the National Health Insurance Scheme;

(n) develop guidelines, processes and manuals for the effective implementation and management of the National Health Insurance Scheme;

(o) ensure the efficiency and quality of services under the national and private health insurance schemes;

(p) protect the interest of members of private health insurance schemes;

(q) Identify and enroll persons exempt from payment of contribution to. National Health Insurance into the National Health Insurance Scheme;

(r) monitor and ensure compliance with this Act and any Regulations, guidelines, policies, .processes and manuals made under this Act; and

(s) Perform any other function conferred on it by this Act or that are ancillary to the object of the Authority.

Box 2: Functions of the National Health Insurance Authority
Source: NHIS Act 852, 2012

In 2004, a revised policy framework was developed. This came about because of the changes that occurred in the development process of the scheme after the passage of Act 650 (MOH, 2004). The revised version brought to focus the concept of the fusion of the Social Health Insurance Scheme and Mutual Health Organizations; it also advocates the concept of cross-subsidization, equity, solidarity and re-engineering of the health insurance system in favour of the poor and underprivileged in society (MOH, 2004). In this regard, the new policy advocates the stratification of society based on the ability to pay. Several stakeholders took part in the discussions during the drafting of the revised national health insurance policy framework. Prominent among them included the Civil Servants Associations, Ghana National Association of Teachers, Ghana Medical Association, the Ghana Police Service, Ghana Employers Association, Social Security and National Insurance Trust, the Trade Union Congress, Institute of Economic Affairs, Civil Society Organization (CSO) and many others (MOH, 2004).

The revised national health insurance policy framework was transformed into the National Health Insurance Regulations, 2004 (LI 1809). L.I 1809 was promulgated in September 2004 to provide operational guidelines for the implementation of the National Health Insurance Scheme. The LI provided detailed guidelines on the registration and operations of the various schemes under the NHIS.

2.2.2. Type of Health Insurance Schemes in Ghana

The law (Act 650) that gave birth to the National Health Insurance Scheme (NHIS) prescribed three types of health insurance schemes in Ghana, these are: (1) District Mutual Health Insurance Schemes, (2) Private Commercial Health Insurance Schemes, and (3) Private Mutual Health Insurance Schemes.

2.2.2.1. District Mutual Health Insurance Scheme (DMHIS)

Under the law that established the scheme, DMHISs were to be established by every administrative district in the country. DMHISs were publicly owned and not-for-profit. District Assemblies were, as part of their performance targets, made to ensure the establishment and registration of DMHISs as a company limited by guarantee under the Companies Act, 1963 (Act 179). According to Seddoh et al. (2011), about 74 per cent of the District Mutual Health Insurance Scheme Offices were set up by their respective District Assemblies, 14.8 per cent by the National Health Insurance Council, and 7.4 per cent were established by Consultants from the MOH while others mentioned include consultants from DANIDA and Traditional Authorities. The law that established the NHIS made it mandatory for the DMHISs to have a governing body, herein referred to as the Board – which shall be responsible for the direction of the policies of the scheme and appointment of employees, including scheme managers and other officers who may be an independent body corporate or committee.

In 2012, the National Health Insurance Act 2003 (Act 650) was replaced with the National Health Insurance Act 2012 (Act 852), which integrates all DMHISs into a unified NHIS. Under Act 852, all DMHISs have been merged into a unitary public health insurer known as the National Health Insurance Scheme, with the National Health Insurance Authority being the regulatory body of all types of health insurance schemes. The revised law maintains the two other types of health insurance schemes – private commercial and private mutual health insurance schemes.

2.2.2.2. Private Health Insurance Schemes (PHISs)

The PHISs are body corporates registered as a limited liability company under the Companies Act, 1973 (Act 179). Acts 650 and 852 prescribed two types of private health insurance schemes in Ghana, which are to be licensed by the Authority. The two types of PHISs are The Private Commercial Health Insurance Scheme (PCHIS) and the Private Mutual Health Insurance Scheme (PMHIS). The PCHIS is for-profit, whereas the PMHIS is mostly not-for-profit. Under PCHIS, premiums or contributions are mostly actuarially determined. The PMHIS is meant for a group of people with a common interest who have mutually come together to cross-pollinate resources with the aim of providing financial risk protection against the high costs of healthcare expenditure for all members of the group.

2.2.3. Membership of the NHIS

All residents of Ghana, including non-citizens, are eligible for NHIS coverage. Both Acts 650 and 852 made provisions for some categories or members of the NHIS to be exempted from contributing to the scheme. By law, the exempted persons are not required to pay premiums and/or administrative fees. For instance, SSNIT contributors, SSNIT pensioners under 18 years of age, and persons 70 years and above do not pay premiums. Expectant mothers and person(s) classified as indigents (the poor class who have no identifiable source of income) are also exempted from paying either premium or administrative fees.

2.2.4. Sources of Financing

The National Health Insurance Scheme (NHIS) is financed predominantly by tax revenue through the National Health Insurance Levy (NHIL). Other sources of funding for the scheme include:

- 2.5% from the Social Security and National Insurance Trust (SSNIT).
- Contributions from members.
- Support from Development Partners (D.Ps).
- Returns on investment.

The NHI levy provides about 74 per cent of NHIS revenue, Social Security and National Insurance Trust (SSNIT) deductions comprise another 20 per cent, and contribution/premium payments provide about 3 per cent. Meanwhile, claims payments account for about 77 per cent of NHIS expenditures (Wang et al., 2017).

The divergent sources of financing the scheme, as enumerated above, somewhat guarantee the financial stability of the NHIS. The use of the NHIL (value-added tax) as the main source of financing the scheme ensures a direct relationship between the country's economic growth and the revenue due to the scheme. Thus, the NHIS revenue automatically keeps pace with economic growth, as is underscored by the stability of NHIS revenue as a share of total government spending (Wang et al., 2017). In the words of Wang et al. (2017), using the VAT to finance health care provides a basis for pooling risks and costs at the national level, which prevents the Scheme from fragmentation experienced by many other countries.

<u>2.2.5. Minimum Benefit Package</u>

The minimum benefit package includes:

- Outpatient services.
- Inpatient services.
- Oral health services.
- Eye care services.
- Maternal health care services.
- Emergencies.
- Medicines published on the Ministry of Health's essential medicines list.

Anecdotally, the benefits package is reported to cover about 95 per cent of all health conditions reported in Ghana's healthcare facilities. That notwithstanding, some health care services are not covered by the scheme; these include rehabilitation other than physiotherapy; vision, hearing, orthopaedic and dental aids and prostheses; elective cosmetic procedures except reconstructive surgery; antiretroviral drugs for treating HIV/AIDS; assisted reproduction, including artificial insemination and hormone replacement therapy.

<u>2.2.6. Payment Systems</u>

Article 37 of Act 852 prescribes that the following payment systems be used to pay a healthcare provider for services rendered to members of the Scheme:

1. Fee for service.
2. Diagnosis-related groupings.
3. Capitation.
4. A payment mechanism that the Board, in consultation with healthcare providers and the Minister, may determine.

At the inception of the Scheme, providers were paid on a fee-for-service (FFS) basis. Due to inequities in tariff and astronomical rise in claims cost, among other reasons, the diagnosis-related-groupings payment method was introduced in 2008 for outpatient and inpatient services while medicine continued to be paid using the FFS arrangement with a predetermined tariffs regime. The capitation payment method was introduced in 2012 on a pilot basis in one of the regions (Ashanti) of Ghana. However, the capitation payment method has since been suspended.

2.2.7. Quality Assurance

The Authority is mandated to ensure that healthcare providers meet a certain basic quality standard to provide the approved package of services to insured members. The process of ensuring that applicant facilities meet a certain basic quality standard to provide the approved package of services to insured members is called credentialing, hitherto referred to as accreditation. Thus, healthcare providers require credentialing certificate from the NHIA before they can provide services to NHIS members.

The law mandates a healthcare provider or health facility to which credentials have been granted to enter into a contractual agreement with the Authority. A provider is granted credentialing for five years at the first instant and subsequently renewable every two years. The Authority is backed by law to deny, suspend or revoke a facility's credentialing, where the need arises.

2.2.8. Administration and Governance

The NHIS law strategically sets out an elaborate governance and administrative framework for the provision of health insurance in Ghana. The Ministry of Health and the Governing Board of the National Health Insurance Authority provide stewardship for the scheme, whereas the NHIA Head Office with its Regional and District Offices is responsible for managing and implementing the day-to-day activities of the Organisation (figure 4).

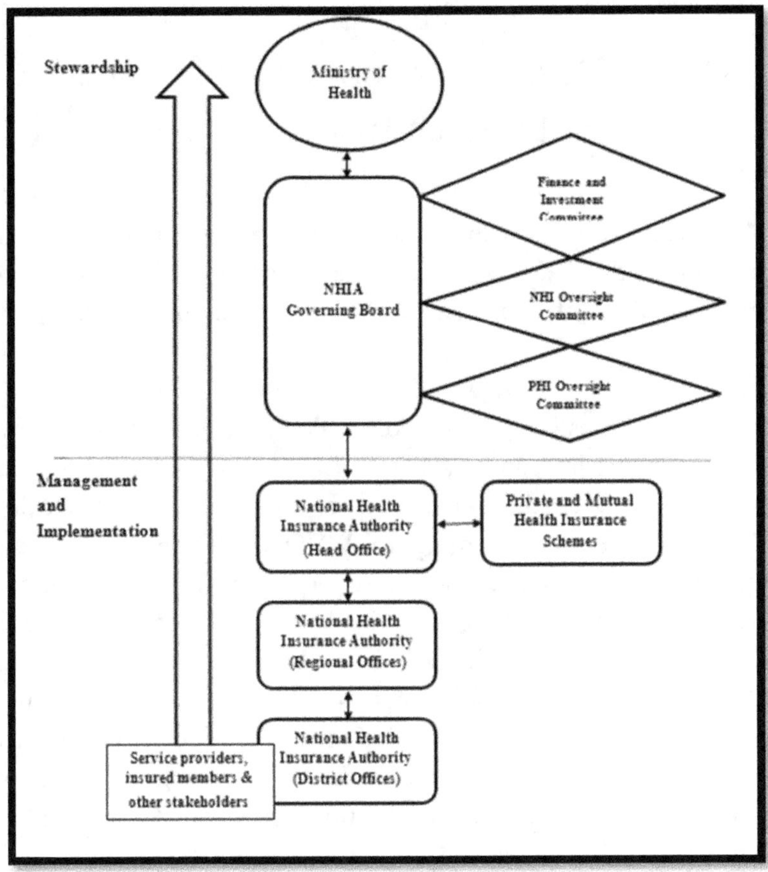

Figure 4: Governance and Administrative Structure of the NHIS
Source: Author's Own Creation

Chapter 3
Policy Design Components of Ghana's National Health Insurance Scheme

This chapter discusses the major policy design components and questions that underpinned the planning, design, and implementation of Ghana's national health insurance scheme.

3.1. Population Coverage

One of the most important policy design components of any social health insurance scheme is how to efficiently and effectively cover the population to attain Universal Health Coverage (UHC). According to WHO, UHC means that all persons can use needed health services (including prevention, promotion, treatment, rehabilitation, and palliation) that are of sufficient quality and effective without being exposed to financial hardship. Whether or not a country will attain UHC for the population depends on the kind of policy design questions regarding population coverage. At the design stage of Ghana's NHIS, several policy design questions on population coverage were posed. These included:

- Which population groups should be covered?
- How can the informal sector be enrolled?
- How should dependents be covered?
- How can the poor and vulnerable persons in society be targeted and enrolled?

3.1.1. Which Population Group Should Be Covered?

The government's vision in instituting health insurance schemes in the country is to guarantee equitable universal access for all residents of Ghana to an acceptable quality package of essential health services without out-of-pocket payment being required at the point of service use (MOH 2004). Membership of the NHIS is open to all persons who are residents of Ghana. By this, all residents of Ghana are required by law to belong to the National Health Insurance Scheme. Based on socioeconomic classifications, membership under the NHIS can be grouped into three (3) main categories: formal sector members, informal sector members and indigents (figure 5).

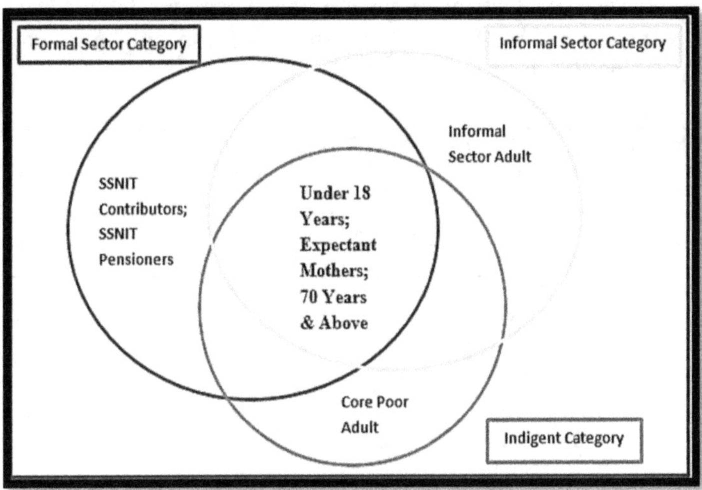

Figure 5: Categories of Members under the Scheme
Source: Author's Own Creation

The formal sector is made up of formal sector employees (including pensioners) and their families; the informal sector is made up of persons working within the informal sector and their families; and indigents – core poor people who are unemployed, who have no visible source of income and do not have any identifiable consistent support from another person.

Some groups of persons (cutting across all three main categories) are exempted from paying premiums (contributions). These groups of persons are called the exempt group, constituting over 70% of the membership of the NHIS. This group is made up of persons classified as indigents and persons belonging to the formal and informal sectors who, for one reason or another, are exempted from paying premium and/or processing fees. The exempt group is made up of children under 18 years of age (dependent); persons in need of ante-natal, delivery and postnatal healthcare services; persons with mental disorders; persons classified by the Minister responsible for Social Welfare as indigents; categories of differently-abled persons determined by the Minister responsible for Social Welfare; pensioners of the Social Security and National Insurance Trust; contributors to the Social Security and National Insurance Trust; persons above seventy years of age; and other categories as may be determined by the Minister (Act 852, 2012). In effect, the only non-exempt group is the informal sector adult (table 1)

Payment-Based Membership Grouping	Pay Premium/ Contribution?	Pay Processing/ Administrative Fees?
Exempt Group		
Indigents	No	No
Persons in need of ante-natal, delivery and post-natal healthcare services	No	No
Children under 18 years (dependent)	No	Yes
SSNIT Pensioners	No	Yes
SSNIT Contributors	No	Yes
Persons 70 years and above	No	Yes
Non-Exempt Group		
Informal Sector Adult	Yes	Yes

Table 1: Payment-Based Membership Grouping Under the NHIS Source: Author's Creation

3.1.2. How Can The Informal Sector Be Enrolled?

With about 70% of the population belonging to the informal sector of the economy, discussions on how to enrol this group into the scheme took centre stage from day one. An address and identification system was developed, which enabled the informal sector to be identified and reached through community and householder status coding patterns. Each individual or household was provided with a unique identification number. The address and identification IDs made reaching out to the large informal sector groups less difficult.

Due to socioeconomic differentials in the sector, the contribution payable by the informal sector adults was graduated based on their ability to pay (Table 2). However, due to the difficulty in determining peoples' income levels, the income-based contribution did not work out as desired. Rather, the DMHISs started to take flat contributions based on the socioeconomic standing of the district, as determined by the Governing Board of that district. For instance, urban areas pay more than rural areas; persons resident in towns and cities that are well-endowed pay more than persons resident in towns and cities that are less endowed.

Grouping	Operational Definition	Contribution (GH¢)	Contribution (US$)[1]
Core Poor	Adults who are unemployed and do not receive any identifiable and constant support from elsewhere for survival	Free	n/a
Very Poor	Adults who are unemployed but receive identifiable and consistent financial support from sources of low income	7.20	0.64
Poor	Adults who are employed but receive identifiable low returns for their efforts and are unable to meet their basic needs	18.00	1.60
Middle Income	Adults who are employed and are able to meet their basic needs	18.00	1.60

---

[1] 1US$=11.27GH¢ on 16/08/2023

Grouping	Operational Definition	Contribution (GH¢)	Contribution (US$)[1]
Rich	Adults who are able to meet their basic needs and some of their wants	48.00	4.26
Very Rich	Adults who are able to meet their basic needs and most of their wants	48.00	4.26

Table 2: Graduated Contribution Amounts Based on Socio-Economic Classification
Source: Adapted From MOH 2004

3.1.3. How Should Dependents Be Covered?

The laws governing the operations of the NHIS made room for the enrolment of dependents in the Scheme. LI 1809 provides that dependents are children less than eighteen years of age. Under regulation 56 of LI 1809, a person under eighteen years of age and both of whose parents or guardians are contributors is qualified to be enrolled on the Scheme and is exempted from payment of contribution. Similarly, a person who is under eighteen years of age and whose parent or guardian has been proven by the Scheme to be a single parent or guardian is qualified to be enrolled on the Scheme and is exempted from payment of contribution.

However, this arrangement was faced with some challenges because some parents or guardians were reluctant to enrol in the Scheme and, by doing so, denied their children equal enrollment in the Scheme (Seddoh et al., 2011). To cure this, the NHIA issued a policy directive in 2009, which decoupled the registration of children with their parents. In effect, all children are allowed to be registered in the scheme whether or not their parents or guardians are insured members. Decoupling the registration of children with their parents was further enforced by the passage of Act 852 in 2012. Consequently, children less than eighteen years of age are registered in the Scheme to enjoy the same benefits package as any other category, whether or not their parents or guardians are insured members.

3.1.4. How Can the Poor and Vulnerable be Targeted and Enrolled?

In accordance with the policy objective that underpinned the establishment of the Scheme, enrollment of the poor and disadvantaged persons in society engaged the attention of the policy designers of the Scheme from day one. To ensure equity in the provision of health care and financial risk protection to poor households, the law provided for the coverage of the poor and vulnerable, herein referred to as indigents, who are exempted from contributing to the Scheme. Regulation 58 of LI 1809 states that a person shall not be classified as an indigent under the Scheme unless that person:

1. Is unemployed and has no visible source of income.
2. Does not have a fixed place of residence according to standards determined by the scheme.
3. Does not live with a person who is employed and who has a fixed place of residence.
4. Does not have any identifiable consistent support from another person.

As part of the registration process and enrolment into the Scheme, officers of the NHIA are mandated by law to elicit the information required as provided above and are supposed to keep the registers of all persons registered as indigents for validation and auditing purposes. Persons identified as indigent enjoyed the same benefits package as any other member or category of members.

3.2. Method of Financing

The fiscal space of any country remains a necessary factor to consider when deciding how to finance any form of social health insurance scheme. In the words of Heller, 2006, fiscal space can be defined as "the availability of budgetary room that allows a government to provide resources for a given desired purpose without any prejudice to the sustainability of a government's financial position". As part of situational analysis at the design phase of Ghana's NHIS, a number of essential policy design questions on the method of financing were posed. These included:

- What is the financial capacity of the country?
- What are the sources of funding to the scheme?
- How sustainable is the means of funding the scheme?
- Should there be co-payment?

3.2.1. What Is The Financial Capacity of the Country?

In response to this policy design question, two key factors remained pivotal - Ghana's financial capacity and the Government's commitment to earmark funds to finance the health sector. Ghana experienced relatively stable microeconomic growth in the early 2000s, and the government used the opportunity to undertake rapid fiscal expansion during this period, which contributed new resources to the health sector. During the period from 2004 to 2008, overall government spending on health increased from 0.93 per cent of GDP to 1.68 per cent (Otoo et al., 2014).

In view of the country's positive financial outlook at the time, among other factors, the government of the day decided to establish a National Health Insurance Scheme, by earmarking a share of the Value Added Tax (2.5%) and taking contributions from the formal sector employees (2.5%) among other sources, with the view to ensuring that the Scheme has good footing and its financial sustainability when implemented, is not put in jeopardy.

In 2001, the Government of Ghana took the decision to join the Highly Indebted Poor Country (HIPC) initiative. The HIPC initiative came with some benefits for the country. In line with government policy, the health sector was selected as one of the beneficiaries of the HIPC funds. The HIPC funds allocated to the health sector were primarily aimed at establishing a National Health Insurance Scheme to replace the cash-and-carry system of healthcare financing (Seddoh et al., 2011). The HIPC funds allocated to the health sector contributed seed capital for the smooth takeoff of the scheme across the country. With support from the central government, every district in the country at the time was tasked to establish a District-Wide Mutual Health Insurance Scheme (DMHIS) for the residents of the district. District Assemblies were mandated to identify promoters to initiate action for the registration of the scheme as a company limited by guarantee under the Companies Act, 1963 (Act 179) for the relevant district within sixty days of the coming into force of Act 650 (Seddoh et al., 2011).

3.2.2. What Are the Sources of Funding to the Scheme?

Ghana's National Health Insurance Scheme is financed through divergent sources (figure 6). These include (1) a 2.5% value-added tax (national health insurance levy) on selected goods and services; (2) a payroll tax contribution of 2.5% of the 17.5% of formal sector workers' Social Security and National Insurance Trust (SSNIT); (3) graduated contributions (premium) from informal sector workers; (4) grants and loans from Development Partners (DPs); (4) contribution from the road accident fund and (6) returns on investment. With time, the financing model varied quite slightly. In the 2018 mid-year budget statement, the government converted the national health insurance value-added tax rate of 2.5% to a straight levy of 2.5% with the aim of increasing the financing frontiers of the NHIS.

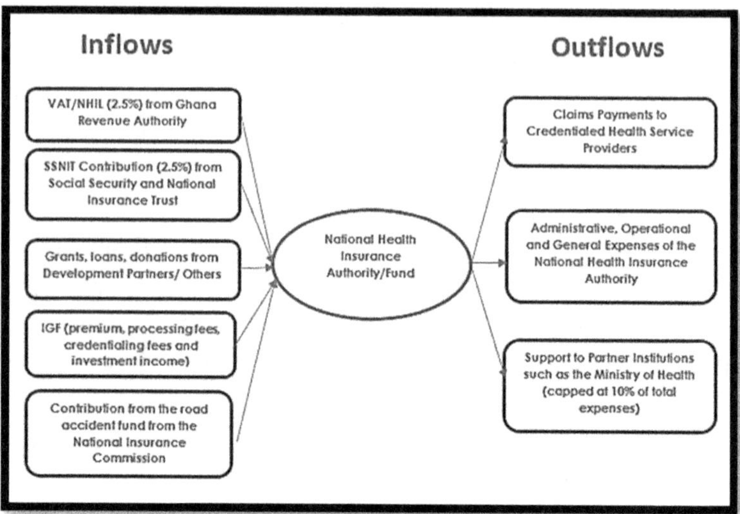

Figure 6: National Health Insurance Fund Flow Structure
Sources: Author's own creation

3.2.3. Should There Be Co-payment?

Ghana's NHIS does not have copayment as one of the financing sources for the Scheme. There is no cost-sharing and/or any form of copayment beyond the approved contributions and/or administrative fees paid by insured members. The nonexistence of copayment as part of the scheme's design and implementation strategies was to encourage and allow as many people as possible to enrol with less or no financial commitment. This was to ensure that money does not become a barrier to accessing the Scheme.

3.2.4. How Sustainable Is the Means of Funding the Scheme?

The sustainability of social health insurance schemes has taken centre space in most technical discourse. As illustrated in Figure 6 above, the designers of Ghana's NHIS decided to have multiple and divergent sources of funding with the aim of making it sustainable. In particular, the earmarking of a share of the VAT (NHIL) and contribution from the formal sector employees from the onset ensured a sustainable and predictable funding arrangement. With this, Ghana's NHIS financing arrangement presents a unique model that pools funds from diverse and progressive sources, thus making the Scheme less susceptible to sustainability threats.

3.3. Risk Pooling and Level of Fragmentation

Risk pooling is the accumulation and management of health insurance premiums so as to ensure that the risk of having to pay for health services is borne by all members of the pool rather than by each affected individual (WHO, 2019). Financial risks associated with health services are shared among all members, not only the affected individual. As part of situational analysis at the design phase of the scheme, a number of essential policy design questions on risk pooling and level of fragmentation were posed. These included:

- Should we have a single or multiple schemes/pools?
- How do we ensure equity and financial risk protection for all?

3.3.1. Should We Have a Single Or Multiple Schemes/Pools?

For the purposes of acceptability, ownership and geo-political considerations, among other factors, Ghana's NHIS started with multiple schemes scattered across the country. The law (Act 650) that gave birth to the NHIS in 2003 decreed the establishment of District-wide Mutual Health Insurance Schemes (DMHISs) in every administrative district. The Act mandates the NHIA to license and regulate the DMHISs. As indicated above, the use of the DMHISs was to promote acceptability and ownership of the Scheme by the citizenry for the smooth takeoff of the national health insurance scheme.

Following the passage of Act 852 in 2012, all the district mutual health insurance schemes were brought together under one umbrella—a unitary public health insurer. This move was in accordance with the policy objective of ensuring cross-subsidization across the various geopolitical districts, which underpinned the establishment of the NHIS. Also, the merger of the multiple schemes was done to avoid fragmentation, have less uncertainty about the occurrence of illnesses, and enjoy economies of scale in administration.

3.3.2. How Do We Ensure Equity and Financial Risk Protection for All?

Ghana's healthcare financing system is progressive, driven largely by the progressivity of general taxes, which make up the bulk of the revenue sources for the national health insurance scheme. Thus, the national health insurance levy, embedded in Ghana's value added tax, is generally reported to be progressive.

Due to the graduated nature of the member's contribution, the NHIS is widely considered to be progressive. For instance, to ensure equity among the informal sector category, contributions are graduated based on the socioeconomic status of the town or city, rural or urban. Also, there is a wide range of premium exemptions. Exempt population groups include all persons aged 70 years and above, retirees who contributed to the Social Security (SNNIT) scheme, all children under 18 years, and indigents – persons who have no identifiable source of income. The exemption covers expectant mothers and persons with mental disorders and categories of differently-abled persons as may be determined by the Minister responsible for social welfare.

3.4. Benefit Package

The minimum benefit package under Ghana's NHIS has been described as 'most generous', covering about 95% of reported health conditions affecting the population (NHIA, 2013). The benefit package is the same for all insured members; the rich, the poor, the young, the aged, male and female, all enjoy the same benefit package. As part of situational analysis at the design stage of the Scheme, a number of essential policy design questions on benefit package engaged the attention of policy formulators; these included:

- Which services should be included in the benefit package?
- Which services should be excluded from the benefit package and for what purpose?
- How should quality assurance be ensured?

3.4.1. Which Services Should Be Included in the Benefit Package?

The prevailing service provision and healthcare infrastructure informed the service provided under the minimum benefit package of Ghana's NHIS. The law provides that to access services under the minimum benefit package under the Scheme, the first point of attendance, except in cases of emergency, shall be a primary healthcare facility, which includes Community-Based Health Planning and Services (CHPS) compound, health centres, polyclinics or sub-metro hospitals and district hospitals. The minimum benefit package includes out-patient, in-patient, oral, eye care, maternity care, and emergency and medicines services published on the Ministry of Health's essential medicines list (box 3).

---

1. Out-patient Services

(1) Consultations including reviews: These include both general and specialist consultations.

(2) Requested Investigations including laboratory investigations, x-rays and ultrasound scanning for general and specialist out-patient services.

(3) Medication, namely, prescription drugs on National Health Insurance Scheme Drugs List, traditional medicines approved by the Food and Drugs Board and prescribed by accredited medical and traditional medicine practitioners.

(4) HIV/AIDS symptomatic treatment for opportunistic infection.

(5) Out-patient/Day Surgical Operations including hernia repairs, incision and drainage, hemorrhoidectomy.

(6) Out-patient Physiotherapy.

---

2. In Patient services
(1) General and Specialist in-patient care.
(2) Requested Investigations including laboratory investigations, x-rays and ultrasound scanning for in-patience care.
(3) Medication, namely, prescription drugs on National Health Insurance Scheme List, traditional medicines approved by the Food and Drugs Board and prescribed by accredited medical and traditional medicine practitioners, blood and blood products.
(4) Cervical and Breast Cancer Treatment
(5) Surgical Operations.
(6) In-Patient Physiotherapy.
(7) Accommodation in general ward.
(8) Feeding (where available)
3. Oral Health services including
(a) Pain Relief which includes incision and drainage, tooth extraction and temporary relief;
(b) Dental Restoration which includes Simple Amalgam Fillings and Temporary Dressing.
4. Eye Care services including
(a) Refraction;
(b) Visual Fields;
(c) A- Scan;
(d) Keratometry;
(e) Cataract Removal;
(f) Eye Lid Surgery;
5. Maternity care including
(a) Antenatal Care;
(b) Deliveries, namely, normal and assisted;
(c) Caesarian Section;
(d) Postnatal care.
6. Emergencies
All emergencies shall be covered. These refer to crisis health situation that demand urgent intervention and include,
(a) Medical emergencies;
(b) Surgical emergencies including brain surgery due to accidents;
(c) Paediatric emergencies;
(d) Obstetric and Gynaecological emergencies including Caeserian Sections;
(e) Road Traffic Accidents;
(f) Industrial and workplace Accidents;
(g) Dialysis for acute renal failure.

Box 3: Minimum Healthcare Benefits Package under NHIS
Source: www.nhis.gov.gh accessed on November 6, 2022

3.4.2. Which Services Should Be Excluded and for What Purpose?

Notwithstanding the above, the law governing the operations of the Scheme specified services that are not covered under the minimum benefits available under the NHIS. Excluded healthcare services include:

- Rehabilitation other than physiotherapy.
- Appliances and prostheses, including optical aids, hearing aids, orthopaedic aids, and dentures.
- Cosmetic surgeries and aesthetic treatments.
- HIV retroviral drugs
- Assisted reproduction, e.g. artificial insemination and gynaecological hormone replacement therapy (box 4).

These healthcare services are excluded because they are considered medically non-essential. Some are vertical programmes being managed by other state agencies. The law allows private health insurance schemes to offer any of these as additional benefits to their members if they so desire.

Rehabilitation other than physiotherapy;
(b) Appliances and prostheses including optical aid, hearing aids, orthopedic aids, dentures;
(c) Cosmetic surgeries and aesthetic treatments;
(d) HIV retroviral drugs
(e) Assisted Reproduction e.g. artificial insemination and gynecological hormone replacement therapy;
(f) Echocardiography;
(g) Photography
(h) Angiography;
(i) Orthoptics;
(j) Dialysis for chronic renal failure;
(k) Heart and brain surgery other than those resulting from accidents;
(l) Cancer treatment other than cervical and breast cancer;
(m) Organ transplantation;
(n) All drugs that are not listed on the NHIS Drug List;
(o) Diagnosis and treatment abroad;
(p) Medical examinations for purposes of visa applications, educational, institutional, driving licence;

(q) VIP ward (Accommodation);
(r) Mortuary Services.

Box 4: Exclusion List
Source: www.nhis.gov.gh Accessed on November 6, 2022

3.4.3. How Should Quality Assurance Be Ensured?

The Authority is mandated to ensure that healthcare providers meet a certain basic quality standard to provide the approved package of services to insured members. Under Ghana's NHIS, the process of ensuring that applicant facilities meet a certain threshold of quality standards to provide the approved package of services to insured members is called credentialing, hitherto referred to as accreditation. Credentialing is a formal process by which the NHIA assesses healthcare providers for compliance with set standards that guarantee quality healthcare to insured members. The overall goal of Ghana's NHIS credentialing system is to promote the provision of quality, safe, efficient and effective healthcare services to insured members (NHIA 2011).

The NHIA, in collaboration with relevant agencies and a multidisciplinary team of health professionals, conducts the credentialing process through inspection of applicant facilities using the NHIS credentialing tools. Facilities that meet the required credentialing standard are issued with credentialing letters – detailing their levels, grades and other contractual conditions. The level and grade of a facility are hinged on factors such as the range of services, environment and infrastructure, equipment, organisation and management, safety and quality management, and human resources.

The law mandates that a healthcare provider or health facility to which credentials have been granted enter into a contractual agreement with the Authority. A provider is granted credentialing for five years at the first instant and subsequently renewable every two years. The Authority is backed by law to deny, suspend or revoke a facility's credentialing. For instance, if a facility fails to meet the minimum requirement, that facility's request may be denied. And where a facility fails to comply with the common management arrangements or memorandum of understanding that facility's credentialing may be suspended or revoked.

3.5. Provider Payment Systems

There is no one-fit-for-all provider payment system or method for all countries. One or more methods can be deployed concurrently. Each method has different effects on the quality of health care services, on efficiency and administration, and on the costs of service provision. According to Langenbrunner et al. (2009), provider payment systems can be powerful tools to promote the development of health systems and achieve health policy objectives. A provider payment system may be defined widely as the payment method combined with all supporting systems, such as contracting, accountability mechanisms that accompany the payment method, and management information systems (Langenbrunner et al., 2009).

In designing the provider payment arrangement under Ghana's NHIS, the questions that engaged the policymakers' thoughts included:

- What type of payment methods should be used?
- Which group and type of service providers should be included?
- How should claims from service providers be managed and paid?

3.5.1. What Type of Payment Arrangements Should Be Used?

Legislative Instrument (L.I) 1809 (2004) defines how providers should be paid under the NHIS. The payment methods specified in L. I 1809 are fee for service, capitation, Diagnosis-Related Groups (DRG), or any other payment system determined by the Minister responsible for health. Since its inception, the scheme has employed three (3) different payment methods: fee-for-service (FFS) for medicines, Ghana Diagnosis-Related Groupings

(G-DRG) for services, and capitation for a defined Primary Care Services (PHC).

Fee for service was the only payment method used by the erstwhile DMHISs. This payment arrangement was faced with challenges. The tariffs used by different DMHISs were not uniform, as different facilities were reimbursed at different rates for treating the same or similar disease conditions, thereby failing to contain costs as desired.

In 2008, the NHIA introduced a standardized service and medicine prices regime. Here, the itemized billing (fee-for-service) system was replaced with diagnosis-related groupings known as the Ghana Diagnosis Related Groupings (G-DRG) payment system, while medicine continued to be reimbursed under the fee-for-service, with a standardized pricing regime. Under the G-DRG payment system, providers are reimbursed the same fixed tariff for cases that fall into the same diagnostic category.

The G-DRG payment system was faced with challenges equally. It could not contain costs, particularly for outpatient services, with outpatient claims accounting for about 90 per cent of total NHIS claims volume and over 70 per cent of total claims costs (Otoo et al, 2014). Also, the G-DRG payment system introduced cumbersome and time-consuming procedures involved in claims processing and adjudication. In response to the above-stated challenges, among other reasons, the NHIA introduced a per capita payment system on a pilot basis in the Ashanti Region in 2012.

3.5.2. Which Groups and Types of Service Providers Should Be Included?

Regulation 22 of L.I 1809 (2004) states that the Council might accredit the following healthcare service facilities to operate under the national health insurance scheme:

(a) teaching hospitals; (b) regional hospitals; (c) district hospitals; (d) quasi-public hospitals (such as the Military, Police, University, and Social Security and National Insurance Trust hospitals); (e) health centres; (f) dental clinics; (g) private hospitals and health clinics; (h) maternity homes; (i) mission hospitals, (j) pharmacies and licensed chemical sellers facilities; (k) private medical diagnostic facilities and (l) such other facilities as the Council may determine.

All the ownership groupings – public, mission, quasi-government and private health service providers can sign up to the Scheme, provided they meet the requisite qualification for credentialing as a health care facility.

3.5.3. How Should Claims from Service Providers Be Managed And Paid for?

Claims management has been a major challenge facing many health insurance companies of many countries in the world, in which Ghana is not an exception. The sustainability of every insurance system depends very much on how well claims are managed. In Ghana, claims are processed using both manual and electronic means. At the inception of the Scheme, the DMHISs processed claims manually. The manual claims processing cycle begins with claims generation by the accredited service provider for services provided to members of the scheme, and subsequently, the claims are submitted to the DMHIS/NHIA within sixty calendar days from the date of the discharge of the patient or the rendering of the service. Fulfilment and vetting of the claims commence thereof. After the vetting, providers are furnished with vetting reports for reconciliations, if any. Finally, if queries are not raised, recommendations are made for payment to be made within four weeks after the receipt of the claim from the healthcare facility.

The Authority may reject or adjust provider claims if it establishes deliberate over-servicing of the patient by the health care facility; unnecessary diagnostic and therapeutic procedures and intervention; irrational medication and prescriptions; fraud; gross and unjustified deviations from current accepted standards of practice or treatment protocols or both; inappropriate referral practices; provision of services other than those for which accreditation has been granted; use of fake, adulterated or substandard pharmaceuticals; use of drugs other than those provided in the National Health Insurance Drug List; false or incorrect information; and the failure of the healthcare facility without justifiable cause to comply with agreement between the Scheme and the health facility.

During vetting, if a claim is established to have material error(s), that claim shall be communicated to the affected service provider within one month after receipt of the claim with a statement of the reason for the rejection or adjustment. The healthcare provider may resubmit the claim after the error has been corrected. However, if the facility is dissatisfied with a decision of the Authority, the affected facility may appeal to the Adjudication Committee established under the law.

To ensure efficiency and effectiveness in claims management, the NHIA introduced electronic claims regime in some selected facilities across the country, with about 90% coverage (NHIA, 2023). Also, the Authority reduced the number of claims processing centers (over 100 at the time) to only four – one for the northern sector; one for the middle belt, while two (2) take care of the coastal sector of the country.

3.6. Governance and Administration

The law that gave birth to the NHIS, Act 650 (2003), strategically sets out an elaborate governance and administrative framework for providing the national health insurance scheme in Ghana. At the development and inception stage, the critical policy design questions regarding governance and administration that engaged the attention of policymakers included:

- How independent should the Scheme be?
- How should the Scheme be regulated and controlled?

3.6.1. How Independent Should the Scheme Be?

The national health insurance scheme is backed by laws Act 650 and Act 852, as amended, thus making the scheme independent of changes in government. The Act established the National Health Insurance Authority as an independent regulator of the National Health Insurance Scheme. The Act further mandates the Authority to establish a National Health Insurance Fund to pay for the cost of health care services to members of the Scheme, establish private health insurance schemes, and to provide for related matters. The NHIA is a delegated agency of the Ministry of Health. The Authority is governed by a Board that reports to the Minister who is responsible for health. The members of the board are appointed by the President, with representations from a wide range of stakeholders including the Ministry of Health (MOH), Ghana Health Service, National Insurance Commission, Social Security and National Insurance Trust, private providers, health professionals with expertise in health insurance, the Chief Executive or a person acting in that office; and two persons, representing members of the National Health Insurance Scheme, one of whom MUST be a woman. The law allows members of the board to hold office for a period not exceeding four years and is eligible for re-appointment for another term only (Act 852).

3.6.2. How Should the Scheme Be Regulated and Controlled?

The Ministry of Health, as well as the Governing Board of the Authority provides stewardship of the national health insurance scheme, whilst the Authority, as an autonomous regulatory body, is responsible for the day-to-day management and administration of the Scheme.

The Authority is headed by a Chief Executive Officer, with three (3) deputies, for (1) operations, (2) administration and human resources and (3) finance and investment. The Chief Executive Officer, as well as the three (3) deputies, are appointed by the President in consultation with the Public Services Commission.

There are several technical directors who head the various directorates and departments at the authority's head office and regional offices. At the district (implementation) level, the authority's functions are performed by district managers, who head the over 150 district offices across the country.

Chapter 4
Performance Assessment of Ghana's National Health Insurance Scheme

This chapter assesses the performance of Ghana's National Health Insurance Scheme (NHIS)—its achievements, contribution to health systems improvement, and financial, administrative, and operational challenges. It further analyses the NHIS's performance in the context of equity, access, and efficiency.

4.1. Achievements

Key achievements of the Scheme included: increased membership enrolment, increased health service utilisation, established state-of-the-art management information systems, established quality assurance and accountability systems, promoted public-private partnership – through credentialing of private facilities, and strengthened stakeholder engagement.

4.1.1. Increased Membership Coverage

Since the full implementation of the national Health insurance scheme in 2005, membership coverage has significantly improved. According to annual reports of the Authority, active membership under the scheme increased to 10.8 million in 2018 from 1.3 million in 2005, representing a significant surge of about 700% growth rate in active membership between 2005 and 2018 (figure 7).

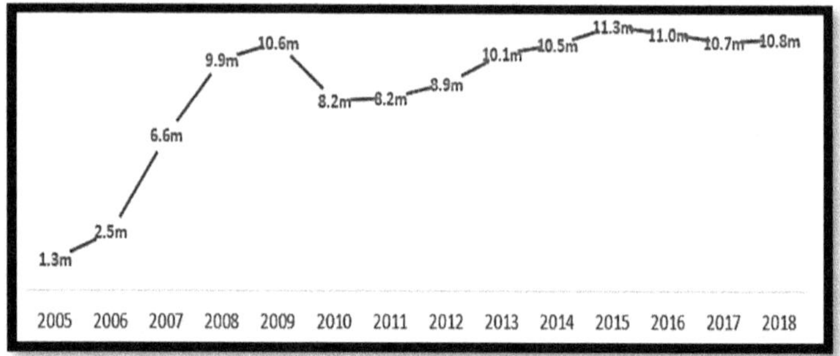

Figure 7: NHIS Active Membership (in million) by year
Source: NHIA Annual Reports 2010 to 2018

Over the past couple of years, national population coverage onto the NHIS has fluctuated, as shown in Figure 8.

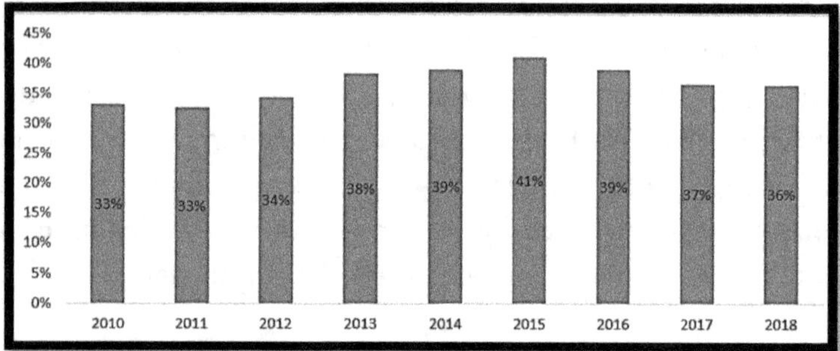

Figure 8: NHIS Population Coverage Trend
Source: NHIA Annual Reports 2010 to 2018

4.1.2. Increased Health Service Utilisation

According to available reports by the Ghana Health Service, the utilization of health services has seen remarkable improvements over the last few years. OPD per capita increased to 0.97 in 2017 from 0.54 in 2005, and the hospital admission rate (per 1,000 population) increased to 52.6 in 2017 from 36.9 in 2005 (Table 3). More than 80% of all OPD attendance is from insured members of the NHIS (GHS, 2016).

Year	OPD Per Capita	Hospital Admission Rate (per 1,000 population)
2005	0.54	36.90
2010	0.98	47.87
2015	1.10	53.70
2017	0.97	52.60

Table 3: OPD per Capita and Admission Rate per 1000 Population
Source: Author's Own Creation with Data Accessed from Ghana Health Services Reports on the Health Sector in Ghana, Facts and Figures (2011 and 2018)

There has been a rise in outpatient service utilisation in Ghana since 2005. From the supply side, the predominant factors that may account for this improvement are the introduction of the NHIS and the Government's efforts in expanding and improving healthcare infrastructure and equipment across the length and breadth of the country. According to the sector ministry (MOH 2022), data on OPD utilisation shows improvement across all levels of healthcare, indicating people's confidence in the healthcare delivery system. In particular, OPD utilisation among insured members under NHIS grew by over 4000% between 2005 (0.60m) and 2018 (27.55m), see Figure 9.

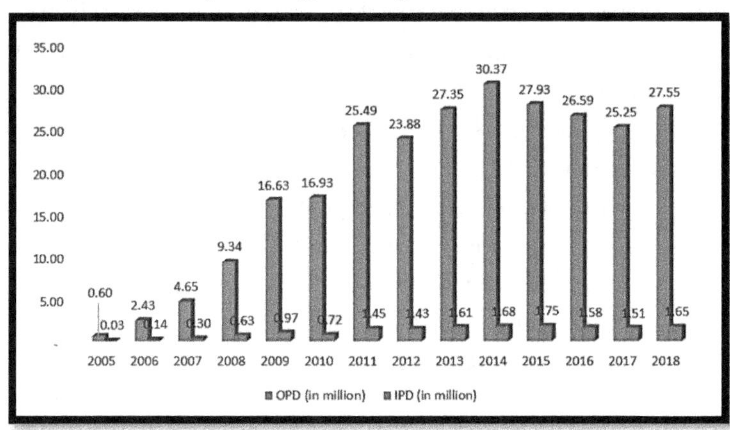

Figure 1: OPD Utilisation and Admissions (In Millions) among NHIS Members
Source: NHIA Annual Reports 2010 To 2018

4.1.3. Established a robust Management Information System

At the inception of the NHIS, the erstwhile DMHISs had different systems that they used for membership and claims management. For instance, the various DMHISs produced laminated ID cards for insured members that were not uniform across the country. In 2007, the NHIA implemented a uniform nationwide magnetic ID card system for enrolled members to address the twin challenges of lack of portability and uniformity with the laminated ID cards. Equally, the magnetic ID card system was faced with challenges such as delays in ID card issuance and distribution and multiple registrations – adversely affecting data integrity.

To ensure the quality of service, data integrity and privacy, the authority progressively invested heavily in building a state-of-the-art management information system comprising hardware and software to manage operational modules such as membership, claims, complaints, quality assurance, finance, audit and human resources.

Over the years, the Scheme has transitioned from issuing a laminated ID card to a magnetic ID card system and eventually to a Biometric and instance ID card issuance System dubbed the Biometric Membership System (BMS). The objectives of the BMS included:

1. Issue instant biometric NHIS membership ID cards to subscribers.
2. Improve the integrity of the membership database.
3. Improve subscriber authentication at healthcare facilities.
4. Generate a unique code (Claims Check Code) for subscribers who access health care and match each claim to subscriber attendance.

In recent years, the NHIS has rolled out a number of innovations and technology-driven initiatives, including mobile renewal systems and the My NHIS App, with the aim of increasing membership coverage, which has stagnated over the last couple of years. Under these systems, members and prospective members can enroll and/or renew their membership online, in the Scheme, in the comfort of their homes and offices, without necessarily having to go to the NHIS registration office. Over the last five years, the NHIS has witnessed consistent improvement in the proportion of the population with active NHIS membership, increased from 10.6 million to 16.8 million between 2017 and 2021 (MOH 2022). This represents a 58.4% growth rate between 2017 and 2021. In particular, the consistent rise in active membership in recent years could be attributed to the introduction of the mobile renewal system in 2018 and a couple of other technology-driven initiatives.

4.1.4. Improved Quality Assurance System

To encourage provider participation at the inception of the Scheme, government and quasi-government health service providers were given blanket [1] provisional accreditation without inspection to provide the approved package of services to members of the Scheme. Private facilities were however granted provisional accreditation based on minimal criteria such as the availability of licensing certificate from existing regulatory bodies.

In 2008, a formal accreditation system was introduced and fully deployed in 2009. Service providers are inspected using standard accreditation tools before being issued credentialing certificates. This aims to ensure that healthcare providers meet a certain basic quality standard to provide the approved package of services to insured members. The law mandates that a healthcare provider or health facility to which credentials have been granted enter into a contractual agreement with the Authority for a period of five years at the first instant and renewable every two years.

4.1.5. Introduced Reforms on Provider Payment Systems and Claim Management

The NHIS has transitioned from the itemized billing (service fee) payment system under the erstwhile DMHISs to a system that is made up of diagnostic-related groupings, fee for service and capitation. In 2008, the NHIA took an important step in reforming the payment system through the introduction of the Ghana diagnostic-related grouping system for services while the fee for service continues to be used for medicines. Then, in 2012, it introduced capitation for Primary Healthcare OPD services on a pilot basis in the Ashanti Region.

To ensure efficiency in claims management, the NHIA has introduced a number of reforms regarding claims management, these included:

1. Establishment of four Claims Processing Centers (CPCs) across the country to receive and process claims.
2. Electronic claims (e-claims) management systems have been introduced in over 90% of health facilities nationwide.

4.2. Health Systems Improvement

This sub-section provides an overview of Ghana's health systems improvement with particular focus on health systems input, health system outcome and health spending.

4.2.1. Health System Inputs

4.2.1.1. Health Facilities

The number of public health facilities in Ghana grew by 41.1%, from 3,011 (2007) to 4,249 (2013) (see Figure 10).

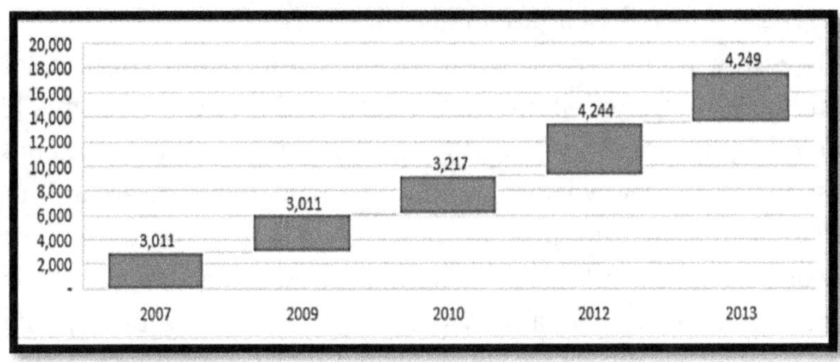

Figure 10: Number of Health Facilities from 2007 to 2013
Source: Author's Own Creation with Data Extracted from Ghana Health
Service Reports on the Health Sector in Ghana—facts and figures (2008, 2011,
2013 2014, and 2015)

Available data from the NHIA shows that the number of credentialed health facilities increased to 4,385 in 2018 from 1,930 in 2009, representing a significant increase of about 127% growth rate between 2009 and 2018. Of the total number of facilities as of 2018, government facilities accounted for about 68%, followed by private facilities at 25%, and faith-based and quasi-government facilities at 6% and 1%, respectively (table 4).

Ownership	2009		2018		Growth Rate
	Number	% Share	Number	% Share	
Government	937	49%	2,982	68%	218%
Private	863	45%	1,096	25%	27%
Mission/Faith-Based	119	6%	263	6%	121%
Quasi Government	11	1%	44	1%	300%
Total (National)	1,930	100%	4,385	100%	127%

Table 4: Credentialed Health Facilities by Ownership
Source: Author's Own Creation with Data Extracted from Published
Annual Reports of the NHIA (2009, 2013 & 2018)

4.2.1.2. Human Resources for Health (HRH)

Providing quality healthcare services and improving health outcomes largely depend on the availability of the right mix of health personnel, especially doctors and nurses. Ghana's essential health worker population has seen a tremendous rise. Thus, in the last decade, Ghana has increased the production and retention of its health workforce, resulting in increases in the health worker (physicians, nurses, and midwives) population density from 1.07 per 1000 population in 2005 to 2.65 per 1000 population in 2017 (GHS 2018).

Although below the WHO standard of 1 doctor to 1000 population (1:1000), the doctor to population ratio improved to 1 doctor to 6,355 persons in 2020, from 1 doctor to 17,899 persons in 2005 (table 5). Similarly, the nurse-to-population ratio has improved from 1 nurse to 721 persons in 2020, from 1 nurse to 1,508 persons in 2005, thus exceeding the WHO threshold of one nurse to 1,000 persons for developing countries.

Indicator	2005	2010	2017	2020
Doctor population ratio	1:17,899	1:10,423	1:8,100	1:6355
Nurse population ratio	1:1,508	1:1,077	1:799	1:721

Table 4: Doctor and Nurse to Population Ratios
Source: Author's Own Creation with Data Accessed from Ghana Health Services (GHS) Reports on the Health Sector in Ghana, Facts And Figures (2008 & 2018) And Holistic Assessment Report of the Ministry of Health 2021.

4.2.2. Health System Outcomes

Ghana has shown considerable improvements in the performance of the health care system in priority areas, such as reducing infant and maternal mortality rates and improving life expectancy at birth. It's, however, difficult to conclude that the introduction of the NHIS is exclusively responsible for these improvements.

4.2.2.1. Life Expectancy at Birth

Life expectancy at birth in Ghana has increased steadily over the years (table 6). In 2000, it was 57.2 years and by 2015 it had reached 62.4 years, representing 9 percentage increase. For the same period, average life expectancy at birth for Africa has increased by about 19 percent, an indication that Ghana's life expectancy is increasing at a slow pace compared to the Africa average.

Country/Region	Year			
	2000	**2005**	**2010**	**2015**
Ghana (GH)	57.2	58.9	60.9	62.4
Africa Average (AA)	50.6	53.0	57.0	60.0

Table 5: Life Expectancy at Birth Ghana and Africa Average
Source: Author's Own Construct with Data Accessed from WHO National Health Accounts Database
Http://Apps.Who.Int/Nha/Database/Select/Indicators/En Accessed on 6th January 2018

4.2.2.2. Infant Mortality

Between 2000 and 2015, Ghana recorded significant reductions in infant mortality rate per 1,000 live births (table 7). During this period, the infant mortality rate reduced by about 34 per cent, from 64.9 in 2000 to 42.8 in 2015. Ghana's institutional infant mortality rate (42.8) is lower than the African average (55.4) as of 2015. The downward trend in Ghana's IMR could be attributed to a number of factors, such as the introduction of the NHIS, the national immunization programme and other child health-related policies and programmes introduced by the Government of Ghana.

Country/Region	Year			
	2000	**2005**	**2010**	**2015**
Ghana (GH)	64.9	56.8	50.2	42.8
Africa Average (AA)	93.7	78.8	64.7	55.4

Table 6: Infant Mortality Rate Ghana and Africa Average
Source: Author's Own Construct with Data Accessed from WHO National Health Accounts Database
http://apps.who.int/nha/database/Select/Indicators/en accessed on 6th January 2018

4.2.2.3. Maternal Mortality

Ghana's maternal mortality ratio (per 100 000 live births) reduced by about 50 percent between the years 1990 (634) and 2015 (319) (table 8). The substantial reduction in maternal mortality ratio over the years could be partly attributed to the implementation of the NHIS's Free Maternal Healthcare Policy (FMCP) in 2008, which exempt expectant mothers from paying premium or contributing to the Scheme.

Country/Region	Year		
	1990	**2000**	**2015**
Ghana (GH)	634	467	319
Africa Average (AA)	965	840	542

Table 7: Maternal mortality ratio (per 100 000 live births)
Ghana and Africa average
Source: Author's own construct with data accessed from WHO National Health Accounts Database http://apps.who.int/nha/database/Select/Indicators/en accessed on 6th January 2018

4.2.3. Health Spending

4.2.3.1. Total Health Expenditure

The share of Ghana's GDP devoted to health has stagnated in the region of 6 percentage points in the last couple of years. Total Health Expenditure (CHE) as a percentage of Gross Domestic Product (GDP) decreased marginally, from 7% (2010) to 6% (2015). Similarly, Domestic General Government Health Expenditure (GGHE-D) as a percentage of General Government Expenditure (GGE) decreased from 10 per cent (2010) to 7 per cent (2015). Ghana's share of GDP devoted to health was higher than the average for some selected comparator countries (figures 11 & 12). Like most of its peers, Ghana has failed to reach the Abuja target of dedicating 15 per cent of the government budget to health.

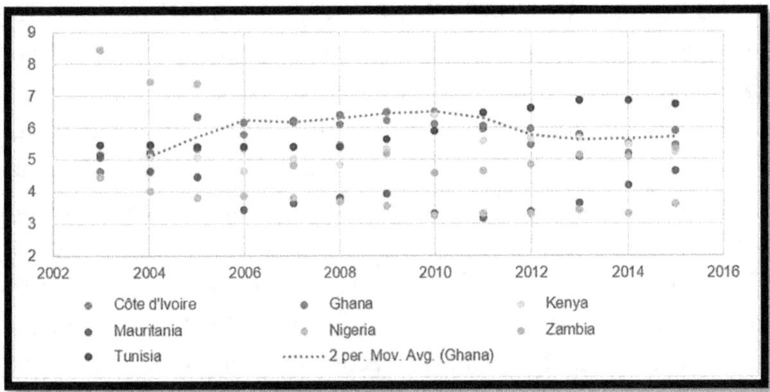

Figure 2: Total Health Expenditure as a Percentage of Gross Domestic Product, Ghana & selected Africa countries
Source: Author's own construct with data accessed from WHO National Health Accounts Database http://apps.who.int/nha/database/Select/Indicators/en accessed on 6th January 2018

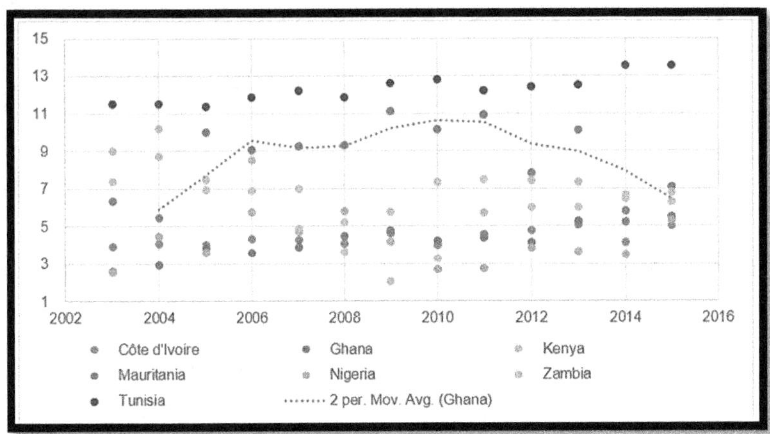

Figure 3: Domestic General Government Health Expenditure as a Percentage of General Government Expenditure, Ghana & Selected Africa Countries

4.2.3.2. Out-of-Pocket Expenditure

Ghana's out-of-pocket expenditure per capita in US$ has decreased from US$ 38 in 2010 to US$ 29 in 2015 (figure 13). The out-of-pocket payment as a percentage of Total Health Expenditure (CHE) in Ghana has decreased from 44 per cent in 2010 to 36 per cent in 2015, higher than the 15–20 per cent out-of-pocket criterion of the World Health Organization. Ghana's OOP as a percentage of current health expenditure was lower than the average for some selected comparator countries (figure 14). The downward trend in OOP spending may be attributed to the implementation of the NHIS in 2004, thus indicating an improvement in financial protection for persons resident in Ghana, especially the poor and vulnerable in society.

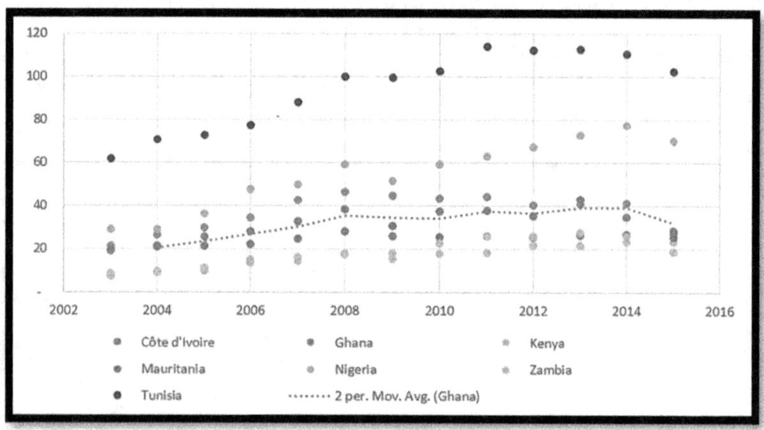

Figure 4: Out-Of-Pocket Expenditure Per Capita in US$, Ghana & Selected Africa Countries
Source: Author's Own Construct with Data Accessed from WHO National Health Accounts Database
Http://Apps.Who.Int/Nha/Database/Select/Indicators/En Accessed On 6th January 2018

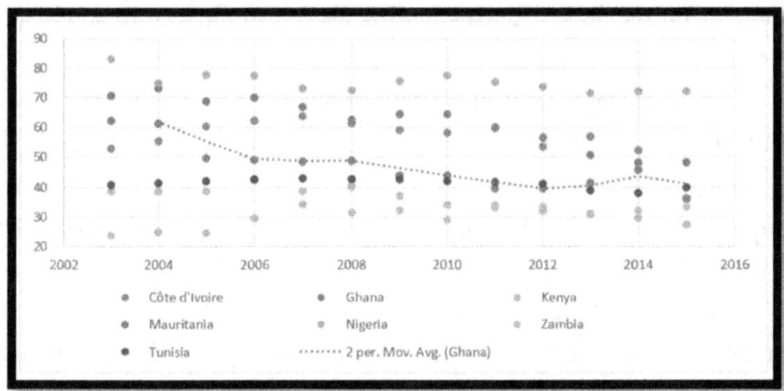

*Figure 5: Out-of-pocket payment as a percentage of Total Health Expenditure
Source: Author's own construct with data accessed from WHO National Health
Accounts Database http://apps.who.int/nha/database/Select/Indicators/en
accessed on 6th January 2018*

4.3. Health Financing System Performance Indicators

This sub-section analyses the performance of the health financing
system in Ghana, with a particular focus on equity, access and
efficiency.

4.3.1. Equity

WHO considers fairness in revenue collection as an intermediate
goal of a health financing system; thus, citizens should contribute
according to their ability to pay. Fairness in government revenue
collection depends on the progressiveness of the taxation system
and other financing mechanisms that the government deploys. In
Ghana, the NHIS is financed mainly from the Value Added Tax
(VAT), representing about 70 per cent of the total income of the
Scheme. Other sources of financing the scheme include
contributions from the informal sector, 2.5 per cent of formal
sector workers' social security contribution, and donor support,
among others. The NHIS funding sources are diverse and largely
progressive. The use of value-added tax as the major source of
funding healthcare in Ghana makes the revenue base for Ghana's
overall health financing system largely progressive (Schieber et
al., 2012). From an equity perspective, enrollment in the NHIS

appears to have led to better utilization of health facilities by the poor.

The minimum benefit package under the Scheme covers about 95 per cent of reported health conditions affecting the population (NHIA, 2013). Regardless of socioeconomic groupings, the rich, the poor, the young, the aged, male and female enjoy the same benefits package without discrimination. The benefit package includes free maternal healthcare services, exempting all pregnant women from paying the NHIS registration fees and contributions. Under the free maternal health care policy, women are entitled to enrol in the scheme free of charge for free antenatal visits, deliveries, and postnatal services.

The Ghana Demographic and Health Survey (GDHS) 2014 report indicated that more than 6 in 10 women (62 per cent) and about half of men aged 15-49 (48 per cent) reported that they are covered by the NHIS. In the same report, 38 per cent of women and 51 per cent of men report that any type of health insurance scheme does not cover them, a sharp decrease from 60 per cent of women and 70 per cent of men aged 15-49 as reported in the 2008 GDHS. The percentage of women and men that the NHIS covers is larger in the highest wealth quintile than in the bottom wealth quintile. 67.2% of women in the highest wealth quintile are covered by the NHIS, and 64.5 are in the lowest wealth quintile. For men, 55.7 per cent are in the highest wealth quintile, and 48.1 per cent are in the lowest (table 9).

Wealth Quintiles	NHIS Coverage (Women)	NHIS Coverage (Men)
Lowest	64.5	48.1
Second	57.6	44
Middle	58.9	40.9
Fourth	61.2	47.9
Highest	67.2	55.7

Table 8: NHIS Coverage by Wealth Quintiles

Source: GDHS 2014

4.3.2. Access

The NHIS continues to provide the relevant social intervention to remove financial barriers to access to health care in Ghana. From an initial active membership of 1.35 million in 2005, enrolment increased to about 10.8 million in 2018 (NHIA 2018). Since the full operations of the NHIS in 2005, health services utilisation has increased significantly across the country. Per capita utilisations for both admissions and OPD have risen considerably. The positive trend in health service utilisation points to the introduction of the NHIS, culminating in improved financial protection and access to health care for the citizenry. According to the 2016 annual report of the Ghana Health Service, total OPD attendance in all health facilities reduced marginally to 29,741,608 in 2016 from 29,949,173 in 2015 and 31,087,824 in 2014. The report further stated that the insured constitute about 82.1% of the total OPD attendance in 2016, compared with 83.1% in 2015 and 83.5% in 2014. Thus, over 80% of OPD attendance at health facilities is by insured members.

Similarly, total admissions in 2016 stood at 1,532,845, out of which 83.3% were insured. The OPD per capita for 2016 was 1.1 and has remained unchanged over the last three years (GHS, 2016). The marginal decline in OPD attendance in recent years has been largely attributed to delays in reimbursement to service providers and their resulting effects.

4.3.3. Efficiency

The NHIS is funded from a number of sources: 2.5 per cent National Health Insurance Levy; 2.5 per cent of each person's 'contribution to the Basic National Social Security Scheme; money that is approved for the Fund by Parliament; money that accrues to the Fund from investments made by the Authority; grants, donations, gifts and any other voluntary contributions made to the Fund; fees charged by the Authority in the performance of its functions; contributions made by members of the Scheme; and money accruing under section 198 of the Insurance Act, 2006 (Act 724) (Act 852). About 70 per cent of NHIS revenue comes from a 2.5 per cent levy added to the value-added tax (VAT), 17.4 per cent from a 2.5 percentage point portion of social security contributions, 4.5 per cent from premiums, and about 5.3 per cent from investment income, grants, and other sources (NHIA 2012).

Earmarking a share of the VAT and social security contributions has been a game changer, resulting in significant and stable revenues for the scheme. The 2012 revision to the law (Act 852) further centralizes the collection of premiums at the national level and, therefore, enhances pooling and standardizes provider payment systems and other aspects of purchasing, making the NHIA a single purchaser managing a single pool of funds (Otoo et al., 2014).

According to Schreiber et al. (2012), the inefficiencies in provider payment systems combined with a generous benefits package, high cost and overutilization of medicines, and operational inefficiencies create an ongoing threat to the Scheme's viability and sustainability. Pharmaceutical spending is another significant source of inefficiency and a threat to the sustainability of the NHIS. Pharmaceuticals account for some 50 per cent of NHIS spending (Otoo et al., 2014). There are major issues concerning not just prices and spending but also quality, prescribing patterns, patient expectations and medicine consumption behaviour (Scheiber et al. 2012).

Over the years, the scheme was characterised by inadequate and delayed inflow of funds from the Ministry of Finance, culminating in incessant delays in the payment of claims to health providers. The average annual percentage of reported collections received by the Authority was 51%, with the remaining 49% received in the ensuing year (NHA 2014). Increases in membership and health service utilisation, with the same funding sources, have resulted in expenditure exceeding income, thereby putting the sustainability of the Scheme under severe threat.

Act 852 introduced a number of reforms in governance, administration, and general operations. One significant feature of Act 852 is the merger of all DMHISs into a unitary public-owned NHIS, which aims to provide enhanced risk pooling with an improved cross-subsidisation mechanism under a single purchaser. Act 852 has provided an integrated three-level administrative system under the scheme. This is comprised of national, regional, and district offices. Under the leadership of the Ministry of Health and the Governing Board of the NHIA, the national office provides leadership and strategic policy direction for the Scheme. The 16 regional offices provide technical support, monitoring and evaluation to district offices and providers within their respective catchment areas.

In contrast, the district offices take responsibility for the implementation of the organisation's programmes, projects and activities. The overall decentralization model of the Scheme faces a number of challenges, such as inadequate resources for the regional and district offices and centralized procurement systems for basic consumables. Centralized procurement arrangements have implications for efficiency. Central procurement for capital-intensive goods would enable the NHIA to obtain better prices through economies of scale. Nonetheless, it must be noted that the decentralized procurement of basic consumables is helpful in fulfilling the immediate needs of the regional and district offices.

4.4. Financial, Administrative and Operational Challenges
Despite its successes, the Scheme is faced with a number of challenges including financial sustainability, problems with identification of the poor, weak information systems, poor quality of care and high cost of pharmaceutical products.

4.4.1. Financial Sustainability

Recent reports suggest that the scheme faces imminent insolvency if measures are not taken to inject capital into its operations. For instance, in the State of the Nation Health Report 2018, authored by the School of Public Health of the University of Ghana, it was suggested that the total expenditure of the scheme has surpassed income, thus putting the scheme in financial difficulties. The scheme's financial challenges could be attributed to escalating claims costs due to extremely high medicine prices, supply and demand side factors, weak referral systems and an 'over-ambitious' benefits package, among others.

Due to Ghana's large informal economy—a characteristic of many developing countries—the Scheme is faced with the challenge of enrolling and mobilising revenue from the informal sector. The difficulty in determining the income levels of informal sector employees continues to pose a barrier to computing the right contribution rate, thereby adversely affecting the scheme's financial fortunes.

4.4.2. Delays in Reimbursement to Health Service Providers

Delays in reimbursement to health service providers continue to be one of the key challenges of the Scheme. On average, service providers' indebtedness to the scheme covers a period of about ten months. In particular, facilities in the rural areas are severely affected by the delays in reimbursement, since close to 100% of their clients are insured members. The erratic nature of claims reimbursement to credentialed service providers affects quality health delivery due to liquidity constraints.

4.4.3. Coverage of the Poor and Vulnerable

Identifying the poor and vulnerable remains a big challenge for most social protection programmes, including Ghana's NHIS. The NHIS has faced the huge hurdle of effectively identifying the poor and vulnerable to be enrolled on the Scheme due to difficulties in identifying them and inadequate resources to reach them—most of whom are staying in hard-to-reach communities. Also, the strict income norm for exempting the poor remains a barrier to enrolment among the marginal poor, who are not able to pay the premium or contribution.

Chapter 5
Policy Options of a Sustainable Health Insurance Model for LMICs

This chapter discusses critical policy design decisions needed for a sustainable, equitable, and progressive health insurance model for low- and middle-income countries.

5.1. Method of Finance

Method of financing has an extremely significant impact on the progressivity and sustainability of a social/national health insurance scheme. Countries that wish to earmark some amount of money to finance the health needs of their population must first and foremost look at their fiscal space and their socioeconomic settings as necessary conditions for takeoff. There is, however, no one-size-fits-all method of financing healthcare. Nonetheless, one of the practical and doable ways of financing healthcare, especially for LMICs, is to increase public funding, generally through taxes, for its health system. To make progress towards UHC, countries must move towards revenue collection by the central government through tax and non-tax sources and prioritise the health sector when doing budget allocation and appropriation.

According to the WHO (2019), "earmarking revenues does not automatically lead to an increase in the level or predictability of public funding for health: more importantly, the political commitment adequately funds the health sector, not whether funds are earmarked". For many LMICs where the informal sector is huge, the most reliable option is to earmark funds through general tax to finance health care. More importantly, levying the population to finance healthcare requires political will, and thus needs the support of all stakeholders especially politicians and Civil Society Organisations (CSOs).

In Ghana, the NHIS is financed through general tax (2.5% straight tax); payroll tax (2.5 formal sector social security contributions); annual appropriation fund (by central government through Parliament); graduated contributions (premiums from informal sector adults); and others such as returns on investment and donations from development partners. Proportionally, about 72.8% of the NHIS revenue comes from general tax; about 17.4% comes from payroll tax; about 4.5% comes from premium contributions; and about 5.3% from investment income, grants, and other sources (NHIA 2012). With this, Ghana's NHIS financing arrangement presents a unique model that pools funds from various sources that is diverse, progressive and less susceptible to sustainability threat.

The use of efficiency gains and co-payments as additional financing mechanisms from the onset of the scheme is critical for a sustainable health financing arrangement. Lack of co-payments and cost-sharing for certain services for non-poor persons is one of the 'downsides' of Ghana's NHIS. LMICs that have yet to establish such schemes are hereby advised to consider cost-sharing and copayment for non-poor persons and patients who self-refer to hospitals or specialists without recourse to primary care. Cost-sharing and copayment serve as (1) an additional source of funding, (2) a cost containment measure and (3) a tool for enforcing the gatekeeper system.

Other options to consider when financing healthcare include the use of health tax (levying tax on cigarettes, alcohol and related commodities) and the use of donor grants. The use of health tax may have varied results, depending on a country's socio-cultural setting. Countries that consume less of these commodities are likely to generate small amounts of additional funds and vice versa. The use of donor grants and supports may be considered for financing healthcare; however, LMICs are advised not to over-rely on donor grants to finance their people's health needs. This may create concerns about sustainability should the donors pull out.

5.2. Risk Pooling

Risk pooling is the accumulation and management of health insurance premiums to ensure that the risk of having to pay for health services is borne by all pool members rather than by each affected individual (Normand et al., 2009). The function of pooling deals with how funds are put together so that individuals do not bear the risk of having to pay for health care. Risk pooling allows for cross-subsidisation between the rich and poor, healthy and sick, young and elderly, and singles and families. The purpose of pooling is to spread financial risk across the population so that no individual carries the full burden of paying for health care.

Ghana's health financing arrangement transitioned from mutual health schemes to establishing district-wide mutual health insurance schemes (DMHISs) in every administrative district as mandated by Act 650 of 2003. As the DMHISs gained acceptability and stability, the government of the day passed a new law (Act 852) in 2012 to merge all the DMHISs into a unitary public scheme. Ghana's health insurance scheme is primarily financed through value-added tax (VAT) revenue. This implicitly means that the central government is directly or indirectly providing sustainable funding for essential health services, which serves as the basis for pooling risks and minimising fragmentation.

The merger of all the DMHISs into a unitary scheme aims to ensure cross-subsidization, equity, solidarity and re-engineering of the Scheme in favour of the poor and underprivileged in society. The merger ensures that the needy in all regions and districts have the same chance to benefit from the Scheme. The 'singularisation' of the Scheme also ensures that deprived districts benefit from the endowed districts through the concept of cross-subsidisation and equity. Ultimately, the merger aims to avoid fragmentation and enhance pooling. The consolidation of the pooling and purchasing functions allows the NHIA to accumulate and manage the resources of the Scheme efficiently and effectively.

Most countries that achieved universal health coverage grew out of mutual health Organisations or community-based schemes, but these evolutions took place over decades (Schieber, 2011). To make progress towards universal health coverage, countries should increase the share of prepaid revenues in the health system and minimise fragmentation in risk-sharing mechanisms.

Countries especially LMICs that are yet to establish national health insurance schemes are advised to start with mutual schemes but with clear-cut framework and timeline from the onset to transition from the multiple schemes to a single scheme or purchaser. The single insurer increases the government's leveraging powers to effectively negotiate with providers and ensure that healthcare services and products are purchased strategically, resulting in efficient use of resources and a reduction in the administrative costs of managing funds.

5.3. Purchasing

According to the WHO, "Purchasing" refers to allocating pooled funds to providers delivering healthcare goods and services to the covered population, per the defined benefit package. Purchasing can be passive (how health services are paid for) or active (how health services are paid for to ensure value for money). The latter is called strategic purchasing. This form of purchasing is preferred because it's evidence-based, defines the service mix and volume, and selects the provider mix in order to maximize societal objectives (Langenbrunner et al., 2009). According to the WHO (2010), purchasing can have a significant impact on health system performance, in particular the efficiency and quality of services, and reducing inequities in service use.

How healthcare providers are paid and remunerated can significantly affect both the cost and the quality of care (Government of Nepal, 2011). Therefore, the use of appropriate provider payment arrangements is critical in the efficient use of available resources. There is, however, no one-fit-all provider payment mechanism. Each method has different effects on the quality of health care services, efficiency, and the costs of services and administration (Charles Normand & Axel Weber (2009)). They further posited that selecting payment methods depends on several significant factors, such as the purchaser's policy objectives and the technical capacity of the purchaser and the provider.

In Ghana, Article 37 of the NHIS Law (Act 852) provides that the following payment systems may be used to pay a healthcare provider for services rendered to members of the Scheme: *(a)* service fee; *(b)* diagnosis-related groupings; *(c)* capitation; or *(d)* a payment mechanism that the Board in consultation with healthcare providers and the Minister may determine. By law, all public or private health facilities, pharmacies and licensed chemical shops are allowed to sign up to the Scheme, provided they meet the prescribed quality assurance and credentialing standards.

Over the years, Ghana has adopted fee-for-service for medicines, GDRG for services and capitation for some selected OPD Primary care services on a pilot basis as the main payment methods. These payment methods have one challenge or the other. Cost containment remains a challenge under both the fee-for-service and GDRG payment arrangements. The G-DRG payment system has failed to contain costs, as desired, particularly for outpatient services, with outpatient claims accounting for about 90 per cent of total NHIS claims volume and over 70 per cent of total claims costs (Otoo et al., 2014).

Similarly, with the FFS payment methods, pharmaceutical spending remains a huge challenge to the sustainability of scheme. Pharmaceuticals account for some 50 per cent of NHIS spending. There are major issues concerning not just prices and spending but also quality, prescribing patterns, patient expectations and medicine consumption behaviour (Scheiber et al. 2012).

In designing payment systems, countries should ensure that the systems so designed have the potential to prevent waste and unnecessary service provision. For a purchaser to be strategic in the services it purchases, it needs information on: (1) which services need to be delivered as a priority? Taking into account the country's burden of disease disaggregated by age, gender and geographical distribution; (2) the cost-effectiveness of the prioritized services; and (3) the country's fiscal space – and government's willingness to allocate resources to the health sector, among others.

Countries, especially LMICs that are yet to establish national health insurance schemes are advised to use capitation and other strategic purchasing instruments as the main payment methods, especially for primary care services. Strategic purchasing functions can be used as a vehicle to attain universal health coverage, especially for primary care, and can serve as a major cost containment tool. Value for money can be enhanced through the introduction of provider payment mechanisms that incentivise providers to scale up the production of services in an efficient manner and improve quality.

LMICs that have yet to establish health insurance schemes may consider preventive and promotive services as a priority area to precipitate their efforts towards UHC. Also, focusing on preventive and promotive services can be a critical claims cost reduction and cost containment strategy for the health purchaser and/or government. For instance, Ghana's benefit package largely focuses on curative services, which drives up claims expenditures. Many preventive and promotive programmes are supported or funded by donors or government vertical programmes. There is therefore the need for the state to consider pooling all the resources under one insurance scheme that will take care of preventive, promotive, rehabilitative, palliative and curative services.

5.4. Stewardship, Governance and Administration

Ghana's NHIS has been strategically designed with an elaborate stewardship, governance and administrative framework backed by laws (Act 650, 2003 (repealed); LI 1809, 2004 and Act 852, 2012 (new)). Act 852 establishes a National Health Insurance Authority to implement a National Health Insurance Scheme; establishes a National Health Insurance Fund to pay for the cost of health care services to members of the Scheme; establishes private health insurance schemes; and provides for related matters.

The NHIA is governed by a board that reports to the minister of health. The MOH together with the governing board provide stewardship functions for the scheme, whiles the NHIA with offices at the national, regional and district levels serve as the managing and implementing officialdoms.

The governing board includes representation of a wide range of stakeholders, including the Ministry of Health (MOH), the Ghana Health Service, the Ministry of Finance, the Ministry responsible for social welfare, the National Insurance Commission, Social Security and national insurance trust, other professionals and experts in health insurance and two persons representing members of the national health insurance scheme. The NHIA is headed by a Chief Executive Officer with three deputies - for operations, finance and investment, and administration and human resources. The Chief Executive Officer (or anyone appointed in that capacity) is an automatic member of the governing board.

Act 852 introduced governance, administrative, and operational reforms, a key part of which integrates all DMHISs into a unified public health insurer, creating a bigger risk pool and resolving some of the governance and administrative challenges under Act 650. Following the passage of Act 852, all the staff of the DMHISs automatically became staff of the NHIA. Given this arrangement, the manpower strength of the NHIA was enhanced. Nonetheless, the large administrative structure, especially at the top leadership level, comes with corresponding high overhead cost implications.

When establishing a social health insurance scheme, countries should ensure that it is strongly backed by law to safeguard it from 'political gimmicks' regarding whether to continue or not whenever there is a change of government. Countries, especially LMICs that have yet to establish national health insurance schemes, are advised to have small administrative structures, especially at the top leadership level, to avoid huge administrative expenses and overhead costs.

References

1) Asenso-Okyere, W.K., Anum, A., Osei-Akoto, I., & Adukonu, A. (1998). Cost recovery in Ghana: Are there any changes in healthcare seeking behaviour? *Health Policy and Planning, 13*(2), 181-188.

2) Atim, C., Grey, S., Apoya, P., Anie, S. J., & Aikins, M. (2001). A survey of health financing schemes in Ghana. Bethesda, Maryland: Partners for Health Reformplus, Abt Associates.

3) Atim, C. (1998). The contribution of mutual health organisation in financing delivery of access to healthcare: Synthesis of research in nine West and Central African countries. Bethesda: Abt. Associates Inc.

4) Atim, C., & Sock, M. (2000). An External Evaluation of the Nkoranza Community Financing Health Insurance Scheme, Ghana. Technical Report No. 50. Bethesda, MD: Partnerships for Health Reform Project, Abt Associates Inc.

5) Carrin, G., & James, C. (2005). Social health insurance: Key factors affecting the transition towards universal coverage. *International Social Security Review, 58*, 45–64. doi: 10.1111/j.1468-246X.2005.00209.x.

6) Carrin, G., James, C., & Evans, D. (2005). Achieving universal health coverage: Developing the health financing system [technical briefs for policy-makers]. Geneva: WHO.

7) Normand, C., & Weber, A. (2009). *Social Health Insurance: A Guidebook for Planning* (Second Edition).

8) Durairaj, V., D'Almeida, S., & Kirigia, J. (2010). Ghana's Approach to Social Health Protection.

Background paper for the 2010 World Health Report. World Health Organization, Geneva.

9) Durairaj, V., D'Almeida, S., & Kirigia, J. (2010). Ghana's Approach to Social Health Protection. Background paper for the 2010 World Health Report. Geneva: World Health Organization.

10) Enyimayew, K. A. (1989). A price to pay: The impact of user charges in Ashanti-Akim district, Ghana. *International Journal of Health Planning and Management, 4*(1), 17-47. https://doi.org/10.1002/hpm.4740040104

11) Enyimayew, K. A. (1988). Financing Drug Supplies of District Health Services in Ghana: the Ashanti-Akim Experience. Harare, Zimbabwe: WHO Workshop on Financing Drug Supplies.

12) Ghana Health Service & Ministry of Health. (2012-2018). *Facts and Figures 2012-2018*. Accra, Ghana.

13) Ghana Health Service. (2016). *Annual Report 2016*. Accra, Ghana.

14) Ghana Statistical Service. (2020). *Rebased 2013-2019 Annual Gross Domestic Product, April 2020 Edition*. Accra, Ghana: Ghana Statistical Service, Statistics for Development and Progress.

15) Ghana Statistical Service. (2021). *National Population and Housing Census Report*. Accra, Ghana: Ghana Statistical Service.

16) Government of Ghana. (2003). *National Health Insurance Act 650*. Accra, Ghana.

17) Government of Ghana. (2012). *National Health Insurance Act 852*. Accra, Ghana.

18) Government of Ghana. (2004). *National Health Insurance Regulations, 2004 (LI 1809)*.

19) Hendriks, R. (2010). National Health Insurance Ghana. Washington, DC: World Bank, and Ghana Ministry of Health, Accra.

20) International Labour Organisation. (2005). *Improving Social Protection for the Poor, Health Insurance in Ghana: The Ghana Social Trust pre-Pilot Project Final Report*. March 2005.

21) Langenbrunner, J. C., Cashin, C., & O'Dougherty, S. (2009). *Designing and Implementing Health Care Provider Payment Systems: How-To Manuals*. Washington, DC: World Bank. http://hdl.handle.net/10986/13806

22) Mensah, J., Oppong, J., & Schmidt, C. (2010). An Evaluation of the Ghana National Health Insurance Scheme in the Context of the Health MDGs. *Health Economics, 19*, 95.

23) Ministry of Health. (1971). *Hospital Fees Act, 1971 (ACT 387)*. Accra, Ghana: Ministry of Health.

24) Ministry of Health. (1983). *Hospital Fees Regulation (L.I 1277) of 1983*.

25) Ministry of Health. (1985). *Legislative Instrument (LI) 1313, 1985*.

26) Ministry of Health. (2004). *National Health Insurance Policy Framework for Ghana, Revised Version*. Accra, Ghana: Ministry of Health.

27) Ministry of Health. (2022). *2021 Holistic Assessment Report*. Accra, Ghana: Ministry of Health.

28) Ministry of Health and Population, Government of Nepal. (2011). *Assessment of the Government Health Financing System in Nepal: Suggestions for Reform*. Nepal.

29) National Development Hent Planning Commission. (2009). *2008 Citizens' Assessment of the National Health Insurance Scheme*. Accra, Ghana: National Development Planning Commission.

30) National Health Insurance Authority. (2011). *NHIS Accreditation in Ghana, Presentation by Dr. Nicholas A Tweneboa, Director of Operations, in Cape Town, 10th March 2011.*

31) National Health Insurance Authority. (2010-2018). *Annual Reports.* Accra, Ghana: National Health Insurance Authority.

32) National Health Insurance Authority (2023): Claims Management Report. Accra, Ghana: National Health Insurance Authority

33) Nyonator, F., & Kutzin, J. (1999). Health for some: The effect of user-fee in Volta Region of Ghana. *Health Policy and Planning, 14*(4), 329-341.

34) Otoo, et al. (2014). Universal Health Coverage for Inclusive and Sustainable Development: Country Summary Report for Ghana. Health, Nutrition and Population Global Practice World Bank Group Report, September 2014.

35) Heller, P. S. (2005). *IMF Policy Discussion Paper, Understanding Fiscal Space.* PDP/05/04.

36) Schieber, et al. (2012). Health Financing in Ghana.

37) Seddoh, A., Adjei, S., & Nazzar, A. (2011). Ghana's National Health Insurance Scheme. New York: Rockefeller Foundation.

38) Sulzbach, S., Garshong, B., & Owusu-Banahene, G. (2005). Effect of National Health Insurance Act in Ghana: Baseline report. Bethesda, Maryland: ABT associates Inc.

39) The Ghana Demographic and Health Survey. (2014). *GDHS 2014 Report.* Accra, Ghana: Ghana Demographic and Health Survey.

40) Vogel, R. J. (1987). *Cost Recovery in the Health Care Sector: Selected Country Studies in West Africa.* Washington, D.C.: World Bank.

41) Waddington, C. J., & Enyimayew, K. A. (1989). A price to pay. Part 1: The impact of user charges in the Ashanti-Akim district, Ghana. *International Journal of Health Planning and Management, 4*(1), 17- 47.

42) Wang, et al. (2017). *Ghana National Health Insurance Scheme: Improving Financial Sustainability Based On Expenditure Review.*

43) World Health Organization. (2009). *An analysis of the health financing system of the Republic of Korea and options to strengthen health financing performance.*

44) World Health Organization. (2019). *Financing for Universal Health Coverage: Dos and Don'ts Health Financing Guidance Note No 9 Conference Copy.*

45) World Health Organization. (2023). Health Financing. Retrieved from https://www.who.int/health-topics/health-financing#tab=tab_1.